Smut's Saga *or* Santa and the Vikings

A pantomime

Richard Lloyd

Samuel French — London
New York - Toronto - Hollywood

© 1994 BY SAMUEL FRENCH LTD

Rights of Performance by Amateurs are controlled by Samuel French Ltd, 52 Fitzroy Street, London W1P 6JR, and they, or their authorized agents, issue licences to amateurs on payment of a fee. **It is an infringement of the Copyright to give any performance or public reading of the play before the fee has been paid and the licence issued.**

The Royalty Fee indicated below is subject to contract and subject to variation at the sole discretion of Samuel French Ltd.

      Basic fee for each and every
          performance by amateurs   Code K
          in the British Isles

The publication of this play does not imply that it is necessarily available for performance by amateurs or professionals, either in the British Isles or Overseas. Amateurs and professionals considering a production are strongly advised in their own interests to apply to the appropriate agents for consent before starting rehearsals or booking a theatre or hall.

ISBN 0 573 16502 5

Please see page iv for further copyright information

SMUT'S SAGA or SANTA AND THE VIKINGS

First produced by Theatre Workshop, Coulsdon, on Saturday, 14th December 1991, with the following cast:

Snorri Snorrisson	Bruce Montgomery
Smut the Smug	Paul M Ford
Big Rollo	Glen Keary and Jonathon Wales
Helga Forkbeard	Rebecca Ford
Eric Big Axe	Mike Brown
Thor Smallsword	Nathan Moughtin
Dame Dustpan	Chris Argles
Tum	Steven Kennick
Dickon	Rachel Handler
Harald	Wendy New
Svein of the Blue Fjords	Tatiana Allison
Filofax	Tim Young
Radish	Kimberley Argles
Stuka	Lisa Boniface
Stoneheart	Richard Lloyd
Santa Claus	Robert Del Toro
Girlie Wimp	Briony Eida
Sundry Vikings	Luke Argles
	Philip Gunstone
	Paul Jones
	Jennifer Lane
	Jo Peck

Director Richard Lloyd
Designer Mark Hobbs
Piano/Keyboards Mark Taylor
Guitars Simeon Dawes
Drums/Percussion Kevin Gibbons

COPYRIGHT INFORMATION

(See also page ii)

This play is fully protected under the Copyright Laws of the British Commonwealth of Nations, the United States of America and all countries of the Berne and Universal Copyright Conventions.

All rights including Stage, Motion Picture, Radio, Television, Public Reading, and Translation into Foreign Languages, are strictly reserved.

No part of this publication may lawfully be reproduced in ANY form or by any means—photocopying, typescript, recording (including video-recording), manuscript, electronic, mechanical, or otherwise—or be transmitted or stored in a retrieval system, without prior permission.

Licences for amateur performances are issued subject to the understanding that it shall be made clear in all advertising matter that the audience will witness an amateur performance; that the names of the authors of the plays shall be included on all programmes; and that the integrity of the authors' work will be preserved.

The Royalty Fee is subject to contract and subject to variation at the sole discretion of Samuel French Ltd.

In Theatres or Halls seating Four Hundred or more the fee will be subject to negotiation.

In Territories Overseas the fee quoted above may not apply. A fee will be quoted on application to our local authorized agent, or if there is no such agent, on application to Samuel French Ltd, London.

VIDEO RECORDING OF AMATEUR PRODUCTIONS

Please note that the copyright laws governing video-recording are extremely complex and that it should not be assumed that any play may be video-recorded for whatever purpose without first obtaining the permission of the appropriate agents. The fact that a play is published by Samuel French Ltd does not indicate that video rights are available or that Samuel French Ltd controls such rights.

CONTENTS

Page	
vi	Synopsis of Scenes
vii	Characters
viii	Musical Numbers
ix	Introduction
x	Dedication
1	*Smut's Saga or Santa and the Vikings*
59	Furniture and Property List
61	Lighting Plot
64	Effects Plot
66	Performing Right Society Notice
67	A Note on Characterization
69	Production Notes
74	Music: "Slushy Duet"
76	Music: "Bash! Bash! Bash!"

SYNOPSIS OF SCENES

ACT I

Scene 1	The hall of Snorri Snorrisson
Scene 2	The sea, somewhere off the English coast
Scene 3	Your town: Dame Dustpan's primitive dwelling
Scene 4	Nearby
Scene 5	Still nearby, but not as nearby as before
Scene 6	Smut's Landing in the frozen north

ACT II

Scene 1	The cave of Helga Forkbeard
Scene 2	The hall of Smut the Smug
Scene 3	The hall of the Mountain King: Stoneheart's lair
Scene 4	The hall of Smut the Smug

CHARACTERS

Snorri Snorrisson, bard and sagamaker
Smut the Smug, a Viking Jarl of wicked disposition
Big Rollo, a giant and Berserk, Smut's incredibly stupid sidekick, played by two persons
Helga Forkbeard, a.k.a. 'Horrible Helga', a hideous witch. Accomplice to Smut
Eric Big Axe, a Viking
Thor Smallsword, also a Viking
Dame Dustpan, an Anglo-Saxon baggage
Tum, Dickon and Harald, wards in the care of Dame Dustpan
Svein of the Blue Fjords, a dashing Viking Prince
Filofax, a person of restricted growth. Servant to Svein
Radish, a beautiful Viking slave girl
Stuka, Commander of Valkyries
Santa Claus, a fat, jolly cove; originally encountered disguised as **Stoneheart**, Lord of the Rock Trolls, King under the Mountain
Girlie Wimp, a regrettably minor role
Viking Bondi, Smut's gang of hooligans

MUSICAL NUMBERS
(See pp.72-73)

ACT I

Song 1		Dame, Eric and Thor
Song 2		Dame, Svein and Filofax
Song 3	Slushy Duet	Svein and Radish
Song 4		Svein and Filofax

ACT II

Song 5	Bash! Bash! Bash!	Dame, Eric and Thor
Song 6		Dame, Svein, Filofax, Santa, Radish, Eric, Thor and Tum, Dickon and Harald
Song 7		All

The licence to perform this play includes permission to perform the two songs listed above and for which the music is printed on pp. 74-76. If you are using other copyright music in this production, please see the Performing Right Society Notice on p. 65

INTRODUCTION

Long centuries divide the epic Norse saga from traditional pantomime, but, surprisingly, the two genres share some similarities. Both are highly ritualized forms of folk entertainment in which time-honoured tales of derring-do, featuring a habitual cast of larger-than-life characters, are performed to delight a deeply involved audience. Pantomime and saga also share many common themes: a journey into uncharted territory; a struggle against overwhelming odds; unequal combat between hero and monster, or hero and villain; and, of course, the capricious intervention of divine or magical powers.

Smut's Saga is an epic Norse saga set in a land of icy fjords and cold, grey seas; a tale of longships and trolls, Valkyries and Valhalla — but expressed in the idiom of traditional pantomime, and through its well-worn cast of characters. Conversely, *Santa and the Vikings* is pure pantomime, incorporating all the essential ingredients of the genre: boundless audience participation, corny *double entendres*, ingenious special effects, men dressed up as women, women dressed up as men, but all with the added bonus of a new story set against the vivid backdrop of Norse myth and with no opportunity missed to exploit every Viking gag or cliché imaginable!

Enjoy yourselves with this script, and your audience will enjoy themselves too!

Richard Lloyd

For Ross

ACT I

Scene 1

Darkness. The low throb of ominous music fills the air. A single spotlight comes up slowly c, illuminating a scholarly man clad in long robes, a huge book open before him. This is Snorri Snorrisson, bard, teller of tales and singer of sagas

Snorri   Long, long ago my children ...

        In time of ice and snow,
        Longships and longswords.
        Long axes, long sagas,
        Smut came to plunder.

        Smut son of Ragnar,
        Ragnar of Thorfinn,
        Thorfinn of Ranald,
        And Ranald of Harald.

        Harald Redhair, Harald Strongarm,
        Late in Valhalla, home of the fallen.

        Harald the fearless, beloved of Asgard,
        Harald whose longships roved the grey oceans.

        Harald son of Halfdan,
        Halfdan of Ruari,
        Ruari of Ranulf,
        And Ranulf of Olaf.

        Olaf Axe-wielder, Olaf Horse-stealer,
        Olaf Shipbuilder, Olaf ...

There is a mighty knock on a gate somewhere below. The sound reverberates before fading away. Gradually the Lights come up

We are in Snorri's hall, which is empty apart from a long table and benches. Furs hang from the timber walls and drape the narrow benches. A chain hangs from the wall. The knocking is heard again

    (*Irritably*) Who is it?
Filofax (*off*) It's me! Filofax!
Snorri What do you want, O Filofax the Dwarf?
Filofax (*off*) I want to come in!
Snorri Go away! I'm telling a saga!
Filofax (*off, whining*) Let me in! It's snowing out here!
Snorri It's always snowing.
Filofax (*off*) And you're always telling sagas! Come on, let me in, will you?
Snorri Oh all right! Hold on a moment.

He pulls the chain and we hear the sound of great timber gates creaking open, off

    Now then. Where was I? Oh yes. (*He resumes his saga*)
        Olaf Axe-wielder, Olaf Horse-stealer,
        Olaf Shipbuilder, Olaf ...

Filofax enters, covered in ridiculously large amounts of fake snow

Filofax Wotcher! (*He brushes the snow from his cloak, shakes out his hood, and stamps his boots*)
Snorri (*coldly*) What?
Filofax Wotcher!
Snorri Look. I'm trying to tell a saga here ——
Filofax Just for a change. What is it this time?
Snorri (*declaiming*) "The Saga of Smut the Smug."
Filofax (*peering at the audience*) They don't want to hear a saga.
Snorri Don't they?
Filofax Nar. They haven't got three days to spare! They want to see a pantomime ... (*To the audience*) Don't you?

Audience participation

Snorri Oh no they don't!
Filofax (*encouraging the audience*) Oh yes they do!

Audience participation

Act I, Scene 1

See. Told you.

Snorri (*changing the subject*) What exactly do you want, Filofax?

Filofax I've come on behalf of my master.

Snorri Ah! Svein, Prince of the Blue Fjords. (*He slips into his saga-telling voice*)

>Svein the Fair, Goldenhair,
>Swift hunter, brave fighter,
>Svein the Ice Lord, Prince of ——

Filofax (*butting in*) Yes, thank you. I know who he is. I don't need the saga.

Snorri (*disappointed*) Oh. Well what does he want?

Filofax He wants your advice.

Snorri (*importantly*) Aha!

Filofax The land of the Blue Fjords sleeps under deep snows. The Frost King's frozen rule lies on the summer country. Glaciers grip the mountains and icebergs close the Fjords. Summer shall never come to the land of the Blue Fjords until Prince Svein takes a wife.

Snorri (*nodding sagely*) Such is foretold in the sagas.

Filofax Yes, well, that's the problem isn't it?

Snorri What?

Filofax Well, the sagas say he has to take a wife, but they don't tell him how, do they?

Snorri Ah.

Filofax The sagas speak of a beautiful princess, but they neglect to mention where he can find her!

Snorri Well, there are plenty of princesses around.

Filofax Yes, but they're all Viking princesses.

Snorri So?

Filofax Well, they're all hideously ugly, aren't they? They look like the Russian Women's Olympic Shot Putt Team!

Snorri Then he must steal a foreign princess.

Filofax (*incredulously*) Steal a foreign princess?

Snorri Yes.

Filofax But he can't do that!

Snorri Why not? He's a Viking, isn't he?

Filofax Yes, but he's not like that. He doesn't agree with stealing. He thinks it's ... dishonest.

Snorri Dishonest? Stealing is a traditional Viking activity. The sagas are full of it! Look, if he doesn't pull himself together and abduct a wife, winter will never leave the country of the Blue Fjords.

Filofax Well, do the sagas say where he has to steal this princess from?

Snorri Where do all Vikings steal from?

Filofax Tesco? (*Or another local shop*)

Snorri England, you idiot! Tell him to journey over the northern sea to find his princess.

Filofax *(dubiously)* England?
Snorri *(emphatically)* England.
Filofax Er... Right. I'll tell him. *(He turns to leave)* Bye then.
Snorri Wait a moment. Don't you want to hear the rest of my saga?
Filofax *(hurriedly)* Um ... no ... Actually I've got to go and watch some particularly interesting paint dry...

Filofax backs out hastily

Snorri Philistine! Now then, where was I? Ah yes. *(He resumes his saga)*
> Smut, son of Ragnar,
> Jarl of the Orkneys,
>
> From Shetland to Samarkand,
> Smut's longships plunder.
>
> Smut the Smug, Smut Hardhand,
> Ravaging coastlines, looting and slaying.
>
> Smut son of Ragnar, crossing the northern sea
> Sailing for England ...

The Lights fade to Black-out

Scene 2

Darkness

We hear the sound of heavy seas and gusting winds. A drumbeat can be heard, growing louder, beating out an insistent rhythm. A weird, shifting light comes up and tendrils of fog blow across the stage. We now discern the bows of a great longship emerging from the mist. The high prow is carved into a fearsome dragon head, beside which Smut the Smug is standing. Helmeted oarsmen labour behind a wall of round shields. Rollo is also present on deck. Great oars dip up and down in unison as the ship moves on to the stage. The oarsmen chant in time to the beat of the drum

Oarsmen *(chanting)*
> War and doom. We bring doom.
> Sword and flame to light the gloom.
>
> War and doom. We bring your doom.
> Fire and steel that spell your doom.

Act I, Scene 2   5

The chanting continues beneath the following dialogue

Lookout (*bellowing*) Land to the west! Land ho!
Rollo (*also bellowing*) Land to the west!
Smut Ship oars! We'll take her in under sail.
Rollo Yes my Jarl. (*He bellows*) Oars inboard, you dogs!
Oarsmen Oars inboard!

As one, the oarsmen ship their oars

Smut (*thoughtfully*) What coast is this?
Rollo The coast of England, my Jarl.
Smut I know it's England, you numbskull! But where in England?
Rollo Uh. Dunno.
Smut Look! (*He points at the audience*) On the beach! A motley herd of snotty-faced churls! They'll soon tell us where we've made land!

Audience participation

> (*Bellowing*) Ahoy there! You lot! Peasants! Do you want your fat heads bashed in by my axe, or do you want to tell me where the nearest settlement is?

Audience participation

> I'm warning you! I am Smut, Jarl of Shetland and Orkney, King of Dublin, Man and the Hebrides, Lord of the Isles, scourge of the northern seas! Answer me to what I ask you, lest I ravage your country and interfere with your women!

Audience participation

> (*Peering at the audience*) By Odin! What an ugly bunch of women! I've seen better looking walrus! With straighter teeth and fewer whiskers too!

Audience participation

> Silence, you snivelling underlings! Shut your flapping cakeholes or you'll get my boot down your throat! Now then! I wish to have a few words with your little ones ... (*He leans down with a sickly grin to address the children in the audience in an oily voice*) Hallo kiddies. It's me. Your old uncle Smut. Well now. Who'd like to come for a little ride in my nice boat?

Audience participation

(*Persevering*) All right, I know! Who'd like a luverly big bag of yummy jelly babies?

Audience participation

(*Losing control*) Who'd like to have their heads bashed in then? And bashed and *bashed* and BASHED! (*He gets a grip on himself*) Bah! You brainless cattle! Just you wait until I land! I'll sort you lot out then! You see if I don't!

Audience participation

Oh yes I will!

Audience participation

Very well! We shall see! (*Shouting to his crew*) Make ready to land! (*He swigs mead from the bleached skull of an enemy*) Sharpen your axes, you sons of Odin! Light your flaming brands and don your warlike helms! Loot and pillage! Ravage and burn! Destroy! DESTROY! DESTROY!

Audience participation

The oarsmen resume their chanting

The Lights grow dim and the longship moves off into the mist

Black-out

Scene 3

England. The Dark Ages

A primitive dwelling wreathed in tendrils of mist

The Lights come up. Three ragged boys race on, chasing the equally ragged Girlie Wimp. One boy (Tum) is short and fat, one (Dickon) is tall and skinny, and the last (Harold) is somewhere in between. The Girlie Wimp screams hysterically as the boys caper around her, jeering and hooting. There is a flurry in the doorway, and Dame Dustpan emerges, a broom clutched in her hands

Dame Oi! What's going on? The audience aren't demanding their money back already, are they?

Act I, Scene 3   7

The hubbub continues unabated

(*Shouting*) Cease firing!

The screaming gets worse

(*Bellowing*) Put a sock in it, you rowdy rabble of runny-nosed ruffians!

Silence

That's better. You interrupted me beauty sleep. Not that I really need it, of course. But you might have caught me in me naughty little lacy negligible! Now then, what's all the hullaballoo, eh?
Girlie Wimp (*snivelling*) It's your horrid children.
Dame Me children? I 'aven't got any children!
Girlie Wimp (*pointing*) Those three! Tum, Dickon and Harald.
Dame Oh them! The three stooges! Yes, well, horrid they certainly are, dear, but they aren't my children, they're adopted.
Tum
Dickon } (*together*) Oh no we're not!
Harald
Dame Oh yes you are! You're me wards. I'm just unlucky enough to be looking after you until you come of age ... if you survive that long — (*she threatens them with the broom*) — which is far from certain! Anyway, I might have known you three would be at the bottom of all this racket. (*To the Girlie Wimp*) What was it this time, dear, demanding yer pocket money with menaces?
Girlie Wimp (*sniffing*) No. They were horrible to me.
Dame Oh, I shouldn't worry about it, dear, they're 'orrible to me all the time — and I'm their keeper!
Girlie Wimp No, I mean really horrible!
Dame They never kidnapped your dolly again, did they? (*Through gritted teeth to Tum, Dickon and Harald*) You haven't chopped the other ear off as well have you?
Girlie Wimp No.
Dame (*taking the Girl aside*) They didn't interfere with — you know — your little fluffy hamster?
Girlie Wimp (*indignantly*) Certainly not!
Dame Oh. Well. Thought it best to make sure. What can be so terrible then?
Girlie Wimp They said that when I grow up ... (*She starts sobbing again*) ... I'd look like you ...
Dame Ah, poor little mite. (*Sympathetically*) And of course you don't ever want to grow up, do you?

Girlie Wimp (*bravely*) Oh I don't mind growing up. (*She starts crying again*) But I don't want to look like you ...

Dame No dear, of course not ... WHAT? What's wrong with looking like me?

Girlie Wimp (*through her tears*) You look like a bloke!

Dame Oooh! I most certainly do not! I'll have you know I'm one hundred per cent woman!

Dickon (*poking the Dame's stomach*) One hundred and fifty per cent more like!

Dame (*ignoring Dickon*) You want to see me in me smalls, my girl, there'd be no doubt then!

Harald Smalls? Don't you mean "extra-larges"?

Dame (*grabbing the girl by the ear*) That's the last time I waste my valuable sympathy on you, young lady! You get along home... (*She shoos the Girlie Wimp off*)

The Girlie Wimp exits

Right! Come 'ere, you three! I want a word with you!

Tum Aw Mum! It was just a joke.

Dame Oh yus?

Tum (*crawling*) Yeah, she'll never look anything like you.

Dame (*flattered*) No?

Harald No. (*Rudely*) She's only got one chin ——

Dickon And no moustache ——

Dame RIGHT! That does it! Hoppit! Go on, get along inside and stay there! Ooooh! Little horrors! (*She shoos the boys off*)

The boys exit

I dunno, the grief I have to endure, ladies and gentlemen. (*She peers at the audience*) Oooooh look! Ladies and gentlemen! Boys and girls! And even ... (*She pulls an expression of extreme distaste*) Brownies! Well! I didn't see you lot lurking down there in the twilight zone. Hallo punters! How are yer?

Tentative audience participation

(*Shaking her head*) Oh dear, oh Lor', that's not very promisin' is it? Look this isn't the (*rival local group*) you know... You are allowed to enjoy yourselves ... Now, let's try again, shall we? I'm going to say "Hallo punters!" and you're going to say "Hallo Dame Dustpan!" All right? After three, then: one, two, three — HALLO PUNTERS!

Audience participation

Act I, Scene 3

Oh yes! That's much better! You nearly woke up the pianist! Anyway, where was I? Oh yes ... Here we are in the Dark Ages, a time when men were men — even though they all wore skirts. 'Ere, d'you know why they called it the Dark Ages?

Audience participation

There is a sudden Black-out

That's why, folks. Dark, innit?

Pause

And it lasts for ages ...

The Lights come up

See what I have to put up with? And that's not the worst of it! We get all sorts of unwelcome visitors knocking on our doors in Dark Age England, and I'm not talking about Jehovah's Witnesses! You name it, and over they come — bloodthirsty barbarians of every denomi-nomi-nom, denomi-nomi-nom — (*she gives up with this word*) — nation. Angles and Saxons, Jutes and Frisians, (*local football team*) supporters — (*pause*) mind you, there's not so many of them ... But worst of all: the Vikings!

There is a dramatic chord

Yes, you may well quake in your corset, Madam! Ooooh, they're such a bloomin' messy race. It takes absolutely ages to tidy up after they've dropped in. They're always breaking things, taking things without askin', setting fire to monasteries, that sort of thing ...

Turn, Dickon and Harald appear in the doorway

Dickon Oi! Dustbin! Can we go out to play?
Dame (*apologizing to the audience*) They're not mine. They're only me wards, y'know.
Harald (*pointing at a member of the audience*) 'Ere, look! There's a bloke down there who looks just like Jabba the Hutt!
Dame (*hastily*) They're no relation, you understand.
Harald (*peering*) He's even fatter than you, Dustbin.
Dickon Cor blimey! Never! No-one's that porky!
Dame Right! That's quite enough lip from you lot of nasty little snotboxes! Why don't you toddle off and find some heavy articulated traffic to play under?

Tum Can we go out then?
Dame Don't see why not, I don't want you under my feet all day. Just you stay out of trouble. And keep an eye open for them dangerous Vikings!
Dickon (*incredulous*) What? In (*local town*)?
Dame And why not in (*same place*) may I ask?
Dickon Blimey! The only dangerous thing in (*same place*) is the (*local curry house, Chinese takeaway, or greasy kebab shop as appropriate*).
Dame They come down river in the night, my lad. Down river and across country. And once they get their big hairy hands on you it's zip! Orf to the frozen north — and not as one of Santa's little helpers. (*She contemplates aloud*) Oh, I shudder to think! An encounter between you three and the dread Vikings —— how terrifying for the poor little dears!
Tum Poo! We're not scared of any old Vikings!
Dame (*darkly*) I wasn't thinkin' of you.
Harald Didn't think you cared about us anyway.
Dame You're absolutely right. I don't. But I wouldn't wish you three on anybody — not even the Vikings!
Tum Oh, thanks very much! (*To Dickon and Harald*) Come on then!

Tum, Dickon and Harald charge off amidst much yelling

Dame (*turning to the audience*) Yes, I know what you're thinkin' folks. You're thinkin': "They can't really be as badly behaved as all that," aren't you? The kids I mean, not the Vikings. Well just you wait and see, that's all ... Just you wait and see ...

Dame Dustpan bustles back into her dwelling

The Lights fade to Black-out

Scene 4

Near Dame Dustpan's dwelling. Eric Big Axe and Thor Smallsword slouch on carrying a sack of booty between them

Thor (*complaining loudly*) Why do we always get looting, eh? Why can't we have a go at pillaging?
Eric Never mind pillaging. What about a bit of ravishing? I notice the boss always handles the ravishing personally.
Thor Mind you, Eric, looting is a tricky business. It takes a really experienced and professional looter to do the job properly.
Eric True enough, Thor. What have we got so far, then?

Act I, Scene 4

Thor Er, let me see ...

They inspect the inside of the sack at some length. Thor looks up

(*Looking up*) Nothin'...
Eric Ah.
Thor Well it's not our fault! Everyone knows that (*local town*) is a right dump! There's nothin' worth nicking!
Eric (*reminiscing*) Not like that time we went on the Majorca expedition, eh?
Thor Nar! That was more like it!
Eric }
Thor } (*together; chanting*) 'Ere we go, 'ere we go, 'ere we go....

Dame Dustpan trudges on, stopping to glare at the two Vikings

Dame Oi! Do you mind? (*She indicates the audience*) This lot have come in here for a kip!

Eric and Thor exchange glances, then vigorously wave their arms and jump up and down, shrieking horribly, to scare Dame Dustpan away

Eric }
Thor } (*together*) Yaaaarrrrrrrrrrgggh!!!
Dame Oh come on. The joke wasn't that bad.
Eric (*perplexed*) Aren't you terrified?
Dame Terrified of what?
Eric Us.
Dame Should I be?
Eric Everyone else is.
Dame Why? Have you got something catching?
Eric (*menacingly*) Do you know who we are?
Dame Give me a clue.
Eric We are rovers ...
Dame Don't you mean BMWs?
Eric (*commencing a heroic saga*) By night we came, from beyond the sea——
Dame 'Ere! You're not illegal immigrants, are you?
Thor Through ice and wind,
Eric Through storm and fire,
Thor In dragon ship of darkest oak,
Eric Of darkest oak our dragon ship,
Thor Across the sea by dragon ship,
Eric High-prowed and sleek, tall-masted, many-oared ——

Dame (*interrupting the saga*) All right, all right! So you came by boat——
Eric Across the icy northern sea ——
Thor From frozen land of crystal fjord and snow-capped mountain ——
Dame (*realization dawning*) Oh, you're Swedes!
Eric No, we're not.
Dame (*hopefully*) Parsnips?
Eric (*irritably*) No.
Dame I've got it! Mangel-wurzels!
Eric We are not root vegetables!
Dame You don't talk like Swedes.
Thor (*interested*) How do Swedes talk?
Dame (*knowledgeably*) Oh, you know. "Splurdy-hurdy-gurdy, Splinky-dinky-doo..."
Eric We are not Swedes!
Dame Danes, then?
Eric No!
Dame All right! Show us your backside!
Eric What?
Dame I bet you've got "Danish" stamped on it!
Thor Of course it doesn't say "Danish" on his bottom ——
Eric (*whispering to Thor*) Phew! You saved my bacon there!
Thor —— it says "I love Mum"!
Dame Oooooh! Saucy devil!
Eric (*to Thor*) Thanks a lot.
Dame All right! I give up. You're not Danes or Swedes —— what are you, then?
Eric (*darkly*) We are Norse!
Dame Norse-e-ating! (*To the audience*) Nauseating! Geddit? Oh never mind.
Eric We are the dread VIKINGS!

Thor and Eric brandish their weapons and gnash their teeth fearsomely

Eric }
Thor } (*together*) Hurrrgha! Hurrrgha Hurgh!!
Dame (*unimpressed*) Is that it then?
Thor Aren't you struck with terror?
Dame Nope.
Thor Why not?
Dame Because I am the dread Dame Dustpan. (*She pulls a hideous face*)

Thor squeals in fright and leaps into Eric's arms

SONG 1
Dame Dustpan, Eric and Thor

Act I, Scene 4   13

Eric (*at the end of the song*) Dreadful indeed!
Dame Thank you.
Eric My name's Eric, by the way.
Dame (*snorting*) Eric? That's not a very dread name is it? Not exactly calculated to strike terror into the hearts of the clergy is it — "Eric"? Eric what?
Eric Big Axe.
Dame (*indicating Eric's war axe*) On account of your enormous chopper, no doubt.
Eric Partly. I also have a big axe.
Dame Yes. Well. (*She hastily changes the subject*) And what's your name, pipsqueak?
Thor I'm Thor.
Dame Why, what have you been doing?
Eric No, no. He's Thor.
Dame Tho? Give him thome ointment.
Thor Not sore! Thor!
Dame Oh! Right! Gotcha! Thor what? Thor head? Thor bottom?
Thor Thor Smallsword.
Dame Smallsword.
Eric (*putting his hands over Thor's ears*) It's because he's got a ——
Dame (*interrupting*) Yes, all right. I think I can guess thank you ...
Eric Look, it's been nice talking, but we've really got to dash because ——
Dame Oh that's all right, I understand. You'd better get on with it then.

Eric exchanges glances with Thor

Eric Er ... Get on with what?
Dame The ravishin'.
Eric (*swallowing*) Er ... ravishing?
Dame Yes. You know. Favoured activity of dread Vikings.
Eric (*hastily*) Oh no, you must be thinking of looting.
Thor (*lightly*) Or pillaging ——
Eric — burning farmsteads ——
Thor — smashing up monasteries ——
Eric — stealing horses ——
Thor (*clutching at straws*) — flower arranging ——

Pause

Dame (*coldly*) And ravishin'.
Eric Er, yes, well, we've got to be going now ——
Dame (*grabbing Eric*) Not so fast, Big Axe ——
Eric But the longship will leave without us!

Dame 'S all right. (*She leers at Eric*) You can stay with me ——
Eric Help!
Thor Look. We're in looting. We don't do much in the ravishing line.
Dame Well, it's high time you diversified!
Eric (*desperately*) Wait a moment! Where's that smoke coming from?
Dame Smoke?
Eric Look! There's a house on fire over there!
Dame 'Ere! That's my slum over there! Some hooligan's set light to it!
Thor Tsk tsk, probably Vikings.
Dame (*releasing Eric*) Well, don't just stand there. Help me put the fire out!
Eric We're right behind you!
Dame Stout lads! Follow me!

Dame Dustpan charges off. Thor moves to follow her

Eric (*grabbing Thor by the scruff of the neck*) Oi! Where d'you think you're going?
Thor To help put the fire out.
Eric What fire?
Thor The house you said was on fire.
Eric That was a diversion, birdbrain! Quick, scarper! Before she comes back!
Thor Before who comes back?
Eric (*shouting*) Grendel's mother! Come on!

Eric and Thor ignominiously turn tail and flee in the opposite direction to that taken by Dame Dustpan

The Lights fade to Black-out

Scene 5

A path near Dame Dustpan's slum. Smut the Smug enters to a chorus of audience participation

Smut (*coming down to the audience*) By Odin! If it isn't that scurvy rabble from the beach!

Audience participation

Shut your gobs, you mealy-mouthed peasants, or I'll slice your flabby tongues out! Oh yes I will!

Audience participation

Act I, Scene 5

Bah! Do you think I care what you maggots say! I'm too busy collecting plunder to waste my breath on a bunch of pimple-brains like you! Anyway, you're only jealous 'cos I'm so rich and good looking! Go on! Admit it! You admire me really, don't you!

Audience participation

Here! I know! How would you like to see what I've nicked so far?

Audience participation

Tough luck! You're going to! (*He bellows*) Bring on the prisoners!

Turn, Dickon and Harald enter, followed by Rollo, prodding them along with his sword and carrying a rubber cudgel. The children wear iron collars around their necks, and all three are linked together by a length of chain

Well, now my little cherubs, how are you feeling? I daresay you're sorry you were so rude to your old uncle Smut now, eh?
Dickon Oh yes, sir. I'd just like to say, sir, on behalf of all of us, sir, how sorry we all are that we were so cheeky to you, sir.
Smut Indeed?
Harald Yes, sir. We don't really think you look anything like the Elephant Man.
Smut No?
Turn No. He's nowhere near as ugly as you.
Smut What!
Dickon Anyway he smelt horrible!
Smut (*suspiciously*) And I don't?
Dickon Oh no. (*Pause*) You smell disgustin'!
Smut What?

Turn, Dickon and Harald blow raspberries at Smut

Rollo! I think a little child psychology is called for!
Rollo Yes boss. (*He starts smacking the children about the head with the rubber cudgel*) Don't be so flamin' cheeky!

There is a sudden flash and bang and Snorri materializes

Snorri Hold!
Smut Eh?
Snorri How dare you strike these defenceless children!

Smut (*perplexed*) Who are you then?
Snorri I am Snorri Snorrisson, bard and singer of sagas. I am telling this saga, and nowhere does it refer to the striking of children.
Smut (*brutishly*) Garn! Push off, Grandad, before I bash you.
Snorri You can't speak to me like that! This is my saga.
Smut Not any more, Dogsbreath! Now shove off!
Snorri (*outraged*) How dare you!
Smut (*to Rollo*) Take these flea-bitten whelps down to the ship, I'll be with you once I've taught this old codger some manners ...

Rollo exits with Turn, Dickon and Harald

(*Advancing on Snorri*) Right! Come 'ere, wrinkle-bonce!

Prince Svein of the Blue Fjords enters with Filofax the dwarf

Svein Hold!
Smut Eh?
Svein How dare you strike that defenceless old gentleman!
Smut (*exasperated*) By Thor and Odin! You can't bash anyone in peace and quiet these days!
Svein I command you to release him this instant!
Smut Well well well! If it isn't Svein the vain! What are you doing here, Pansy Potter? Collecting wild flowers?
Svein Still up to your old tricks, Smut?
Smut Just doing my bit for the Scandinavian economy, your Highness.
Svein By terrorizing the old and weak?
Smut Absolutely. Somebody's got to do it. You've obviously forgotten what it means to be a Viking!
Svein I haven't forgotten. I have simply learned that stealing and bullying are wrong!
Smut Toffee! You're just a big softie, Svein! A snivelling cowardy-custard! Well the gods won't be saving you a seat in Valhalla!
Svein If Valhalla is full of robbers and thieves like you I couldn't care less!
Smut Bah! Just get out of my way, unless you want my axe in your gob!
Svein You don't frighten me. Now, on your way, before I am forced to teach you a lesson in manners.
Smut Ha ha ha ha! I'm not scared of you! (*To the audience*) I'm not scared of him!
Filofax (*hiding behind his master*) Oh yes you are!
Smut (*outraged*) Oh no I'm not!

Audience participation

Act I, Scene 5

Svein (*drawing his sword*) Very well, let us put the matter to the test of steel. Prepare to take your seat in Valhalla!
Smut (*hastily*) Hang on! I've just remembered. (*He pulls a rather girlie-looking diary out of his furs and flicks through the pages*) I've got a very important appointment!
Svein (*peering over Smut's shoulder*) Oh yes? Where?
Smut (*snapping the diary shut on Svein's nose*) Anywhere! Goodbye Prince Svein, cockroach brain! I'll get even with you! Just see if I don't! Ha ha ha ha!

He runs off

Snorri (*sagely*) I fear he is right, my Lord. Nonetheless I am most grateful for your assistance.
Svein (*gingerly fingering his nose*) Oh, it is no trouble, good father. I am glad I was able to help.
Snorri Smut is a bad sort. He has abducted three local children, and carried them back to his ship.
Svein Do not fear. They shall come to no harm. I will see to that!
Snorri You are a brave and noble Viking. Let me offer you something in return. A gift for Svein the valiant. (*He produces a fur-wrapped parcel*)
Svein Oh really, sir. There is no need. (*His curiosity gets the better of him*) What is it?
Snorri It is a horn, wrought in precious metals by the gods of old. If you should ever find yourself in grave danger, blow upon the horn ...
Svein (*unwrapping the parcel and staring at the horn*) But why? What do you mean?
Snorri I am sorry, my friend, I can stay no longer. I have intruded long enough. But remember — only blow upon the horn in the direst danger——
Svein But wait...
Snorri Farewell, Svein the Fair, Goldenhair. (*He glances off stage*) Someone is coming, I must go now. May good fortune accompany your quest!

There is a flash and a bang and Snorri vanishes

Filofax (*aside*) Flash git.
Svein (*regarding the horn*) This is all very well, but I'll never remember to use it ...
Filofax What about asking this lot to remind you? (*He gestures to the audience*)
Svein Yes! What a good idea! (*To the audience*) Will you help me?

Audience participation

You will? Oh good! Right then, well, when you see that I am threatened by direst danger, will you shout out to me?

Audience participation

Very well. You must shout "Svein, Svein, blow your horn! Live to see another dawn!" Will you do that for me? All right then, let's have a practice after three. One ... Two ... THREE!

Audience participation

That wasn't bad, but you must shout loudly enough to shake the snow from the mountains, then I will know that truly I am in direst danger! Shall we try again? One ... Two ... THREE!

Audience participation

Dame Dustpan enters

Dame My word! You Vikings aren't half a noisy bunch! I mean isn't murderin', pillaging and wreaking havoc enough? Do you have to shout all the time as well?
Filofax Ooooh! You look magnificent when you're angry — give us a kiss!
Dame Gerroff! I'm not surrendering me virtue for a snog with an Ewok!
Filofax (*undeterred*) What about a brief fling?
Dame Certainly. I've always wanted to try me hand at dwarf throwing!
Filofax (*dodging*) Aha! Playing hard to get are you?
Dame Listen, mush! I've had quite enough of dread Vikings for one day! And you can tell your pals Eric and Thor that I've got a bone to pick with them!
Filofax Eh?
Dame They told me that me slum was on fire and then did a bunk.
Svein (*intervening*) I must apologize if we or any of our countrymen have disturbed your peace, madam.
Dame Ooooh, I say! Hoity-Toity! (*To the audience*) Look out, girls, I think I'm about to score! (*She adjusts her bosom and turns back to Svein*) Hallo Cheeky! Who are you then?
Svein I am Svein, Prince of the Blue Fjords.
Dame (*excited*) Really? I had a blue Fjord once.
Svein Indeed? With clear waters and deep?
Dame No, with furry dice and a vinyl roof.
Svein I don't understand.

Act I, Scene 5

Dame It was a blue Fjord Cortina! Boom Boom! (*To the audience*) A Ford Cortina, geddit! Oh, go back to sleep!
Svein (*drily*) I see.
Dame Anyway, what can I do for you, your horniness?
Svein I seek a girl of extraordinary beauty...
Dame (*aside*) Ooooh! I think it's my lucky day! Now don't tell me — her hair the colour of odd darned socks!
Svein (*dreamily*) Her hair the colour of spun gold ——
Dame Just like mine before I had it transplanted! Her eyes the indescribably murky hue of cold, greasy washing-up water!
Svein — her eyes the clear blue of the summer sea ——
Dame 'Ere! My eyes are blue — underneath the black...
Svein The blood of an ancient royal house will run in her family ——
Dame Yes, well, noses run in my family...
Svein — in short, I seek a Princess of the English.
Dame (*disappointed*) Oh. Well you're out of luck, pal. We used to have a princess, but she was carried off by the Vikings when she was but a tiny babe.
Svein Ah! How was this child called?
Dame How was she called? Well, er... sort of — (*she assumes the vacuous expression of an adult gurgling to a baby*) — coochie coochie coo, who's a lovely little sprog then?
Svein No no no! How was the child named?
Dame Oh, now, let me see ... I know! It was ... er ... something to do with fields ...
Filofax Cowpat?
Dame I've got it! Meadowsweet!
Svein (*entranced*) Meadowsweet!
Dame That's it! Meadowsweet.
Filofax (*sourly*) I prefer "Cowpat".
Svein (*wistfully*) Meadowsweet ... What a lovely name ...
Dame Oh she was a lovely little pudding all right. I bet she's a real corker now!
Svein (*with resolve*) I must find her!
Dame You'll be lucky mate! She was nabbed by your lot of hairy hooligans fifteen years ago ... (*Hastily*) Not that I remember much about it, of course; I was only a mere slip of a girl meself at the time ...
Svein Would you recognize her?
Dame (*dubiously*) Well ... I dunno ... shouldn't think so ...
Svein But there's a chance ...?
Dame Well ... p'r'aps ...
Svein How would you like to take a voyage in my dragon ship? The adventure of a lifetime, a journey to the winter lands beyond the icy Northern Sea?

Dame Ooooh! You're never going to overpower me, radish me, and carry me off to satisfy your animal desires are you?
Svein (*taken aback*) Certainly not.
Dame (*disappointed*) Oh. Well. In that case I'll stay put.
Svein But ...
Dame No buts. The sea air don't agree with me; you wouldn't want diced carrot all over your nice clean boat, would you?
Svein But ...
Dame Anyway. I have to see to me wards ...
Filofax (*conversationally*) I had a wart once ...
Dame Not warts, wards!
Svein Your wards?
Dame Turn, Dickon and Harald.
Svein Ah.
Dame Ah, what?
Svein I fear I have grave news for you.
Dame Grave news? Oh, I'm dying to hear it! Boom Boom!
Svein Your wards have been abducted by the evil Jarl Smut the Smug.
Dame (*horrified*) Abducted? What, you mean carried off by the Vikings?
Svein (*gently*) I'm afraid so.
Dame (*aghast*) Not spirited away over the sea to Viking land?
Svein Very probably.
Dame And I'll never see them ever again?
Svein (*with compassion*) I'm afraid not.
Dame (*heaving a sigh of relief*) Thank Gawd for that!
Svein What?
Dame I've been trying to get shot of the little stinkers for ages — old Mug the nut can have 'em for a few days. Let's see how he copes!
Svein But they are your wards!
Dame Wards? Listen, pal! Those three are a fully-fledged casualty department on the move! (*To the audience*) Wards! Casualty department! Geddit? Oh, never mind ...
Svein You are responsible for their welfare ——
Dame Poo! They can look after themselves.
Svein And if Smut should harm them?
Dame Stuff 'n' nonsense! Smut harm them? He'll be lucky if he lasts the week!
Svein (*gravely*) He will sacrifice them to Stoneheart.
Dame Stoneheart?
Svein Lord of the Rock Trolls. King under the Mountain. Stoneheart rules the domain where Smut has his lair. And the troll's price is human blood ...
Dame It is?
Svein Oh yes. Smut pays his rent in captured children who are offered up to satiate the troll's lust for warm, sweet blood.

Act I, Scene 6

Dame Ooooh! How 'orrible! Well I'm not having that, my lad! If you think I've spent the best years of me life raisin' those little brutes just to provide a light lunch for some animated boulder you've got another think coming!
Svein So! You will come with me?
Dame Eh?
Svein I will rescue your wards from Smut's clutches, if you will help me to find the Princess Meadowsweet!
Dame (*reluctantly*) Oh all right! I suppose so. Just keep Ronnie Corbett here away from me ...
Svein Agreed.
Dame Agreed? Bloomin hecky! What have I let myself in for?

SONG 2
Dame Dustpan, Svein and Filofax

They exit

Black-out

SCENE 6

Lapland — Smut's Landing

The villain's lair in the frozen north. The dragon ship lies moored alongside a rickety wooden quay. Nearby, a snow-laden hall nestles behind a sturdy timber palisade. The jagged peaks of high, white-capped mountains rise in the background. Smut is on the quay supervising his men, who are unloading booty. Eric and Thor are busy on the ship; Rollo stands guard over Turn, Dickon and Harald

Smut (*shouting at Eric and Thor*) Tie up aft, you lubbers! And look lively! Rollo! Bring those prisoners ashore! If they give you any cheek, bash 'em!
Rollo Yes, my Jarl!

Rollo hustles Turn, Dickon and Harald — all looking somewhat unsteady — on to the quay

Smut (*bellowing*) Radish! Radish! Where has that accursed girl got to?

Radish runs on. She is young and pretty, although raggedly clothed and somewhat begrimed

Radish (*out of breath*) I'm here, my Jarl.
Smut And where have you been?

Radish In the kitchens, my Jarl.
Smut Sleeping in front of the fire, I daresay!
Radish No, my Jarl! I have been cleaning the ovens.
Smut Bah! Don't give me that! You're a lazy little good-for-nothing! Well, it's the woodshed for you tonight, my girl!
Radish Oh no! Please! Not the woodshed! It's so cold! I'll freeze!
Smut Ha ha ha ha! The woodshed! And count yourself lucky I let you keep your rags!

Audience participation

> In the meantime, clean this ship out! These filthy pups couldn't hold down their gruel! (*He turns to Tum, Dickon and Harald*) Well, my pretty chickens, welcome to Smutland! How do you like it?

Tum It's c ... c ... c ... cold.
Dickon M ... m ... miserable.
Harald And ... squ ... squ ... squalid.
Tum M ... m ... m ... much like yourself.
Smut Ha ha ha ha! Never fear, you'll be warm soon enough! I have a luncheon appointment tomorrow in the hall of the Mountain King. And guess what's on the menu? Ha ha ha ha! You won't feel nearly so cold once you're roasting on a spit over Stoneheart's fire! Ha ha ha!

Audience participation

> Ah! Shut up you lemmings! Come Rollo! Back to my hall for a jug of warm mead! (*To Eric and Thor*) You two clowns! Stay here and guard the prisoners! Walk them around to clear their heads! I don't want them puking in my hall!

Eric (*gloomily*) Yes, my Jarl!

Smut and his men traipse off through the snow and exit into the hall, leaving Eric, Thor, Radish, Tum, Dickon and Harald staring awkwardly at each other

> (*Uncertainly*) Er ... right then ... Well, you'd better walk around a bit or something then ...

Radish (*reproachfully*) Oh Eric! You're not really going to make these poor children do exercises. Can't you see how exhausted and terrified they are?
Eric Well ... er ...
Thor Yeah. Come on, Eric. Have a heart!
Eric (*defensively*) Look! I'm only obeying orders!
Radish (*changing tack*) You must be frozen yourself, poor thing! Why don't you go to the kitchens? Cook's got a pan of stew on the fire.

Act I, Scene 6

Eric What sort of stew?
Radish Reindeer, I think.
Thor Cor! My favourite! Come on, Eric, let's go!
Eric (*wavering*) But what about them?
Radish Oh don't worry about them. I'll make sure they're all right. I'll bring them up to the hall in a minute.
Eric Really?
Radish Of course. (*She smiles at him*) You'll have finished your stew by then.
Eric (*smacking his lips*) Oh, er ... right then. Well, we'll see you in a minute. C'mon, Thor.

Eric and Thor trudge off

Radish (*as soon as they have gone; to Tum, Dickon and Harald*) Quickly! We must hurry!
Tum (*alarmed*) Why? Where are we going?
Radish Do you want to be served up as dish of the day tomorrow?
Tum Ugh! No fear!
Radish Right then! Listen carefully. This is Troll Mountain. Stoneheart's hall is on top. But there's an old man who lives on the other side of the mountain. I don't know who he is, but I met him once when I was rounding up the goats. He seems very kind. You must go and find him. I'm sure he will give you shelter until the snows thaw and you can escape from Smutland.
Dickon But how are we going to find him?
Radish I'll show you the start of the path around the mountain. Follow the path and you'll find him.
Harald Why are you helping us?
Radish (*valiantly*) Because I cannot stand by and watch the wicked Smut send more innocent children to Stoneheart's grisly table.
Harald But what will he do to you when he finds you've helped us to escape?
Radish He can't treat me any worse than he already does, can he?
Harald No, I suppose not. He's pretty horrible to you, isn't he?
Radish He's horrible to everyone.
Harald But he's especially horrible to you.
Radish Well, I am only a slave.
Harald Oh, yes, there is that.
Radish We must go, before they come back!

They exit R. *Svein and Filofax enter* L

Svein (*whispering*) This is Smut's lair right enough. Look, there's his longship.

Filofax (*loudly*) What in Asgard are we doing here? You must be potty! Everyone knows Smut is a right head-case!
Svein Shhhh! I promised Dame Dustpan that I would rescue her wards. Then we can start looking for ... (*He sighs wistfully*) Meadowsweet.
Filofax Yuck!
Svein Wait! Where's Dame Dustpan? We've lost her!
Filofax You can't lose something that big! She's still on the boat, honking up her breakfast.
Svein Well, go and fetch her! She might wander off and get lost.
Filofax Fat chance.
Svein I thought you liked her.
Filofax After three days at sea? She was constantly either yakking or chuckin' up. Tell you the truth, I couldn't tell the difference after a while!
Svein Yes, well, just go back and fetch her.
Filofax But, Boss ...
Svein At once.
Filofax All right, all right, I'm going. Don't get yer knickers in a twist!

He exits L, *Radish appears* R

Radish (*seeing Svein*) Oh! Er ... hallo.
Svein (*jumping*) What? Oh! Hallo. Who are you?
Radish Radish.
Svein Radish?
Radish It's not my real name. That's what Smut calls me.
Svein Ah.
Radish I'm only a slave, you see. Who are you?
Svein Er ... Svein.
Radish Are you a slave?
Svein No. I am a ... er ... a simple merchant adventurer.
Radish You don't look much like a merchant.
Svein You don't look like a slave.
Radish But I am. (*Sadly*) And nothing can change that.
Svein You never know — Smut may come to a sticky end.
Radish (*glumly*) And I may never be free.
Svein They can only own your body, Radish. Not your heart, and not your mind. (*He takes her hand*) You can be as free as you want, on the inside.

SONG 3
Slushy Duet
Svein and Radish

Radish   We are two golden, ripening, swaying sheaves of sweet love

Act I, Scene 6   25

                    Waiting to be reaped by the scythe of togetherness.

                    We are two honey-laden bees, just brimming with love,
                    Making sweet hearts of gold in the air, full of happiness.

                    Cupid's oiling up his bow with golden treacle, silver syrup
                        and joy,
                    As the sugar sweetly drips into our hearts combining you
                        and I.

                    The angel in the sky with a twinkle in his eye,
                    He makes the brightest stars shine out
                        I love you.

Svein   Cupid's oiling up his bow with golden treacle, silver syrup
                        and joy
                    As the sugar sweetly drips into our hearts — combining
                        you and I.
Radish   The angel in the sky with a twinkle in his eye,
                    He makes the brightest star shine out.
Both   I love you.
Radish (*as the song ends; speaking*) Who are you? What are you doing here?
Svein I am looking for someone. Someone special — a princess ...
Radish (*releasing his hand*) Oh. I see. Where will you find her?
Svein I — I do not know — I will not know her until I find her ...
Radish Ah. It will not be easy then.
Svein (*awkwardly*) It will be harder now ...
Radish (*turning away*) I am sorry.
Svein I also seek three others. Children kidnapped from the lands beyond the northern sea. Are they here?
Radish (*after a pause*) No. No they are not here.
Svein Oh. Then I must search elsewhere. (*He turns to go*)
Radish No, wait! (*Hesitantly*) I have sent them up the mountain — to save them from Smut.
Svein You need not fear. I have sworn to rescue them. Will you show me which way they went?
Radish (*her mind made up*) Of course. Come with me.

They exit R *as Filofax and Dame Dustpan tramp on* L

Dame Gordon Bennett! Come on, you lousy leprechaun! Where is he then? Where's the lovesick frog got to now?
Filofax Blowed if I know. He was here a moment ago.

Dame Bloomin' heck! Don't tell me you've dragged me across the snowy wastes right into the enemy's penalty area, only to find our centre-forward has done a bunk?
Filofax Look, he's about somewhere. He's probably gone off for a quick scout.
Dame Has he indeed? Disgustin'! And I thought he was such a nice young Viking.
Filofax So, what shall we do while we're waiting? 'Ere ... (*He winks*) What about a bit of wallop?
Dame I'll give you wallop in a minute, you hideous little hairy half-pint!

Radish runs back on R, stopping in surprise when she catches sight of Dame Dustpan and Filofax

Radish More visitors!
Dame (*jumping in fright*) Eeeek! Blimey! You gave me a fright! Ooooh, I've gone all clammy in me camisoles!

Filofax grabs her as if to verify this; she slaps him

(*To Radish*) Just who might you be, young lady?
Radish I'm Radish. Who are *you*?
Filofax (*impressively*) We are the companions of his Royal Self-Importance Prince Svein of the Blue Fjords. Have you seen him?
Radish *Prince* Svein? Why he told me he was a simple merchant adventurer!
Dame Well it was partly true, dear.
Radish He is an adventurer?
Dame No, he's simple.
Smut (*bellowing off*) Radish! Where are you?
Radish It's Smut! Quickly! You must hide!
Dame Hide? I'm not hiding from him! (*To Filofax*) We're not afraid of him are we?
Filofax No, we're not afraid of him! (*Pause*) We're flamin' terrified! (*He leaps into the dragon ship and ducks out of sight*)

Smut strides on, followed by Rollo, Eric and Thor

Smut You! Girl! Where are my prisoners?
Radish They ran off, my Jarl! I couldn't stop them!
Smut You allowed them to escape? (*He catches sight of Dame Dustpan and does a double-take*) And who is this ... this ... stranger?
Dame Blimey! I can't be stranger than you, mate.
Smut (*suspiciously*) What's going on here?
Dame Who knows? It's the plot. (*To the audience*) Far too complicated if you ask me.

Act I, Scene 6

Smut (*acidly*) Who is this?

Eric and Thor exchange glances

Does anyone know her?
Eric (*mumbling*) Er ... no.
Smut No?
Eric (*resolutely*) Never seen her before in me life.
Dame (*waving coyly*) Hallo Eric!
Smut (*rounding on Eric*) Are you acquainted with this quivering lump of whale blubber?
Eric Well, actually...
Smut (*shouting*) I will not have loose women brought into my hall!
Dame 'Ere! Who are you calling a loose woman? There's nothing loose on me, mate — just a few bits sagging, that's all! (*She adjusts her bosom*)
Eric (*protesting*) She's nothing to do with me! She must have stowed away on the ship!
Dame (*improvising*) Oh Eric my husband! How can you tell such awful porky-pies?
Smut Husband? (*Incredulously*) This fat drab is your wife?
Eric She's making it up! I could never be married to that!
Smut No?
Dame No. (*Bleakly*) I've got too much taste.
Smut (*roaring*) Silence you revolting, leprous pustule of feculence!
Dame (*bristling*) 'Ere! You can't speak to me like that!
Smut Why not?
Dame Because I don't know what it means.
Smut I'll have you know that I sit upon "The Thing".
Dame Yes, well, no wonder you've got that stupid grin on your face then ...
Smut (*grating*) "The Thing" is the Viking Assembly.
Dame Oh well, "Things" ain't what they used to be ...
Smut (*thundering*) Be quiet! You shall be subject to my will!
Dame (*moving to slap Smut*) Ooooh! You filthy little man! You keep your will to yourself!
Smut (*rounding on Radish*) And as for you, slave, you shall pay dearly for your treachery! (*He leers*) Stoneheart will be satisfied, and as you have allowed his lunch to escape, *you* shall take their place!
Radish Oh no!
Dame (*indignantly*) 'Ere! You can't feed Radish to no troll!
Smut And why not?
Dame You'll give him wind. (*To Eric*) Very indigestible radishes are ... (*To the audience*) Oh, they play awful havoc with me downdraught! (*She wafts her voluminous skirts*)

There is a suitable sound effect

Smut Take her! Lock her in the woodshed!
Dame Ooooh! Take me too! Lock me in the Woodman! (*Or local hostelry*) Preferably the public bar!

Audience participation as Radish is seized by Eric and Thor and carried off struggling

Smut (*pointing at Dame Dustpan*) And bring her to my hall. I can find work for her in the kitchens for now: tomorrow she shall accompany me to the hall of the Mountain King. (*He leers at Dame Dustpan*) I shall make a gift of you to Stoneheart! How do you fancy becoming his bride?
Dame How do you fancy a biff on the hooter?
Smut Ha ha ha! I can see it now! The troll's wife! The troll and his *trollop*! Ho ho ho!
Dame Never mind trollop. You're off your trolley, pal! I'm getting out of here!
Smut Wait!
Dame Oh! You rude man! About sixteen stone, since you ask.
Smut You shall be prepared for Lord Stoneheart's pleasure in the traditional Scandanavian manner! (*To Rollo*) Take her to the sauna!
Dame (*fuming*) Ooooh! I'm going to get very steamed up in a minute!
Smut Followed by a plunge in the icy pool ...
Dame Get off! I'll get permafrost in me petticoats!
Smut Then roll her around in the snow and thrash her with a bundle of birch twigs.
Dame You are a very sick man.
Smut It's an old Viking custom.
Dame (*shouting*) You need therapy, pal.

Dame Dustpan is dragged off by Rollo

Smut Ha ha ha ha! Wonderful! Stoneheart will be pleased! And those three scurvy brats won't get very far in the snow! I wonder if the frostbite will get them before the wolves do? Ha ha ha ha!

Audience participation

Oh ho! You can bleat all you like, my little seal pups, but it won't help your friends! Nothing can save them now! Ha ha ha! Things are going rather well for me, aren't they?

Audience participation

Oh yes they are!

Act I, Scene 6

Audience participation

Well just you wait until the second half! Then you'll see! Ha ha ha ha!

He sweeps off to audience participation

After a moment Filofax peers over the edge of the dragon ship. He looks nervously around before clambering out

Filofax By Loki! That's torn it!

Svein enters R, stamping the snow off his boots

Svein Hola! Filofax!
Filofax Oh master! Something terrible has happened!
Svein Don't tell me Dame Dustpan has been seized by the wicked Smut the Smug and is to be married to the dreaded troll Stoneheart on the morrow!
Filofax All right, I won't.
Svein Oh. Well what happened to Radish?
Filofax (*darkly*) Tonight the woodshed. Tomorrow the casserole.
Svein (*purposefully*) We must rescue her!
Filofax Must we?
Svein Of course! She is a brave, courageous, not to mention quite beautiful girl. She helped those children to escape from Smut.
Filofax Oh yeah? Where are they then?
Svein Somewhere up the mountain. I followed their tracks for a while, but the snow came on again so I turned back.
Filofax (*gloomily*) They've had it then.
Svein I think not. I fancy we shall find them later. Now, however, I must apply my mind to planning the timely rescue of Radish and Dame Dustpan, the overthrow of the wicked Smut the Smug, and the demise of the fearsome troll, Stoneheart!
Filofax (*drily*) That's not going to leave us much time to locate Princess Cowpat is it? When are we going to do all this then?
Svein (*clapping him on the shoulder*) After the interval of course!
Filofax Oh! That's all right then.

SONG 4
Svein and Filofax

If desired, other characters can appear and join in the song, as this is the end of Act I

Lights fade to Black-out

CURTAIN

ACT II

Scene 1

Before the main tabs. A solo spot comes up on Snorri Snorrisson, who reads aloud from his great book

Snorri (*intoning*) And so, my children, as you have seen these things, so they have come to pass.

> Smut son of Ragnar, his captives imprisoned,
> Travels this day to the top of Troll Mountain.
> But what news of rescue?
> Where is Prince Svein the Fair?

A Light comes up on the other side of the stage illuminating Svein and Filofax, who proceed to mime to Snorri's commentary

> Trollslayer! Goldenhair! Where is Prince Svein the Fair?
> Counselled by Filofax, trusted companion,
> Not to face Smut's men in heroic combat.
> "I know a better way, I know an easier way,
> I know a safer way", promises Filofax.

During the following passage, Filofax looks increasingly indignant, and eventually abandons his miming altogether

> Filofax cunning mind, Filofax wily hand,
> Filofax faint heart, Filofax yellow streak!
> Scared of his shadow, afraid to ——

Filofax (*interrupting*) 'Erol Hang on a minute! Hang on a minute! (*To Svein*) Are you going to let him talk about me like that?
Svein (*sourly*) Why not? It's true, isn't it? I should never have listened to you. (*He paces up and down*) I should have hammered on Smut's gates with my sword, challenged him to single combat, and liberated his captives. *That* is the Viking way.
Filofax (*amazed*) *That* is the way to get your head kicked in, chum! Single

Act II Scene 1

combat? Do you really think Smut's whole gang were going to stand idly around while you gave their guv'nor a good pasting? Not likely! We'd have been fish food, mate! Chopped up faster than you can say pickled herrings!

Svein (*unconvinced*) Hmmmph! Well, what's your plan then?

Filofax We shall seek the advice of one who can tell us exactly how to get the better of Smut—even though his gang outnumbers us by twenty to one. (*Pause*) Well, twenty to one-and-a-half.

Svein Who?

Filofax (*peering around conspiratorially*) None other than Helga Forkbeard.

Svein Not Horrible Helga the witch?

Filofax (*bridling*) And why not?

Svein She's potty!

Filofax Apart from that.

Svein What do you mean "apart from that"? She's barking mad! Not to mention completely untrustworthy!

Filofax Ah! But she knows a thing or two, though.

Svein Yes — about creating mischief and causing trouble! She's an even bigger menace than Smut!

Filofax She should be able to tell us how to sort him out then, shouldn't she?

Svein (*dubiously*) Well, I don't know ...

Filofax It's got to be better than taking on Smut's whole crew with only me behind you.

Svein Yes, and about five miles behind me probably. Where is Helga's secret lair?

Filofax (*mystically*) Ah! Deep in hidden caves, high in the far mountains.

Svein It sounds an awfully long way away.

Filofax Not really. (*He gestures*) Just behind the curtains, actually ...

Snorri (*interrupting irritably*) Ahem! Do you mind? When you've quite finished, I'd like to get on with my saga.

Svein Sorry. Carry on.

Snorri Thank you. Now then, where was I? Ah yes. (*He resumes his saga*)
        Svein, brave fighter, Filofax, yellowbelly,
        Journeying northward, into far mountains,
        Seeking the witch lair of Helga Forkbeard,
        Horrible Helga, Helga the hideous,
        Worker of magic, devious sorceress ...

The Lights fade on Snorri

The CURTAINS *open to reveal the cave of Helga Forkbeard. It is a dark chamber cluttered with crude timber furniture. Rows of bottled potions share crowded shelves with stacks of ancient, dusty books and jars containing weird, pickled specimens of flora and fauna. A magic circle is painted on the floor and a barrel with a skull and crossbones on it stands nearby. The cave is littered with empty gin bottles, and what appears to be a filthy mound of ragged clothing (actually Helga Forkbeard) is deposited on the floor to the rear. Svein and Filofax enter cautiously*

Svein *(whispering)* By Odin! What a tip!
Filofax *(sniffing)* And what is that disgustin' smell?
Svein Isn't that you?
Filofax Certainly not!
Svein Oh. Makes a change.
Filofax Well, this is her place right enough. Look at all this stuff. She's got more noxious potions than The Body Shop ...
Svein *(looking around)* But where is Horrible Helga?

Sinister music plays as the festering heap of discarded clothing behind them begins to move

Audience participation

(*Looking round*) What's behind me? There's nothing there...

Audience participation

Oh no there isn't!

Audience participation

Is there? Where? What, that pile of mouldering old rags?

Svein nudges Filofax, who goes reluctantly to investigate

Helga *(leaping up with a scream)* YAAAAARRRGGGGHHH!
Filofax *(yelping)* Help! Mercy! Please!
Svein *(grabbing him)* Don't panic! It's only old Helga.
Filofax What do you mean, don't panic? I've just discovered where the pong's coming from!
Helga *(cackling madly)* Har har har! Well boys! What do you know!
Svein Er ... Pardon?
Helga Watcha want then, Gorgeous? Something to get rid of a troublesome dwarf? Har har har! I can do you a nice unguent to keep the midgets away!
Svein Repellent.

Act II Scene 1

Helga Yes! That's it.
Filofax He was talking about you.
Helga Oh. (*Slightly taken aback*) Har har har!
Svein Er ... Actually, we have come for some advice.
Helga (*conversationally*) Oh well, fire away. You know what they say — "A problem shared is a problem immediately spread round the whole neighbourhood!" Har har har! (*She cackles through the following line*)
Svein Very well. Our problem is Smut the Smug.
Helga (*stopping in mid-cackle*) Ah.
Svein Can you help us?
Helga (*guardedly*) P'r'aps. What's it worth?
Svein Er ... My eternal gratitude?
Helga (*leering*) Not quite good enough.
Svein Well what then?
Helga (*taking him aside*) Tell you what: I'll take the dwarf off yer hands.
Filofax (*in alarm*) No!
Svein Er ... no, I don't think so ——
Filofax (*hastily*) He'd be lost without me. I'm his personal organizer, you see.
Helga Okey-doke! (*She turns to go*) You can see yourselves out
Svein Wait! (*He considers*) I could let you have a case of gin.
Filofax (*helpfully*) Why don't you let her have a case of bubonic plague?
Helga Gin! Well why didn't you say so? Now you're talking my language! Har har har!
Svein So how are you going to help us?
Helga Well now, let's see ... (*She consults a huge motheaten book*) Hmmm ... What about a spell of enchantment to render you impervious to sword blows?
Svein (*cautiously*) That sounds all right.
Helga Very well, come and stand over here then, within the magic circle inscribed on the floor.

Svein stands where directed

(*Crooking a finger at Filofax*) And you, my hairy little friend. Might as well do you at the same time. Fifty per cent extra free eh? Har har har! (*She turns away and busies herself with her bottles and jars*)
Svein (*under his breath*) I don't like this.
Filofax Now what's the matter?
Svein I smell a rat.
Filofax It's her. I told you. You should have offered her a case of disinfectant ...
Helga (*turning back to them*) Right then. Here we go ...

As she intones the following, she puts the ingredients mentioned into a small stone bowl at their feet

"Leaf of woodbine, bark of yew,
Sap of hemlock and superglue,
Mix with essence of lotus flower
(*Suddenly shouting*) To bind them in a spell of power!"

There is a Black-out, then a blinding flash! When the smoke clears, Svein and Filofax are trapped in a shaft of green light from overhead. They mime trying to push their way out, encountering an invisible wall all around

(*Triumphantly*) Har har har! Gotcha!
Svein (*outraged*) What are you doing? I command you to release us this instant!
Helga (*cackling*) Hony-Baloney! Har har har!
Svein (*resigned*) Oh, very well, you win, you can have the dwarf.
Filofax (*horrified*) Master!
Helga (*sneering*) I don't want the dwarf! Nasty, ugly, mange-ridden little furball! I want you! And now I've got you! Har har har!

Audience participation

Svein (*tentatively*) Er ... does this mean you're not going to help us defeat Smut the Smug then?
Helga Me? Help you defeat Smut the Smug? You mean Smut, my oldest and dearest crony? Smut who went to the same borstal as me? Smut who is a fellow member of the (*local town*) Round Table?
Svein (*covering his eyes*) Oh no!
Helga Oh yes! Har har har! And it just so happens that I'm off to see him very shortly. We have some very important business to transact.
Svein What sort of business?
Helga (*nastily*) My business! (*She can't resist gloating*) Let's just say it involves some of this stuff! (*She hoists up the barrel marked with a skull and crossbones*)
Svein What is it?
Helga It's called "gunpowder" dearie, and it blows things up. I flogged a few barrels to Smut. Once he has feasted in the hall of the Mountain King today, he intends to rid himself of his tiresome landlord once and for all! BOOM! Shredded troll! No more Stoneheart! Har har har!
Svein But Dame Dustpan will be up there! And Radish!
Helga Then they'll all be splatted together, won't they? Smut's got enough powder to take the top off that mountain like it was a boiled egg! Har har har!
Filofax (*aside*) That's no yolk.

Act II Scene 1

Helga Har har har! Be seeing you suckers! Smut will be pleased to know I've got you safely under lock and key! Har har har!

She bustles out, cackling

Svein (*calling*) Hey! Wait!
Filofax (*gloomily*) It's no good! We've had it! If Smut doesn't do for us, the smell will!
Svein Never mind us! What about the others? Smut's treachery is going to get them all blown to Asgard! Poor Radish. Poor Dame Dustpan.
Filofax Poor us, stuck here, doomed to suffer this horrible niff!
Svein (*considering*) Filofax, there's no doubt about it, we now find ourselves in a situation of direst danger.
Filofax (*agreeing*) Oh yes, definitely a situation of direst danger.
Svein What on earth are we going to do?
Filofax I don't know. (*He appeals to the audience*) What on earth can we do in this situation of direst danger?

Audience participation. The audience may just about remember the correct words (see p. 18)

Get the horn? I really don't think this is the time or the place to ...
Svein (*excited*) Yes! That's it! The horn! I shall sound the horn of the Old Gods! (*He pulls the horn from his pouch and unwraps it. Raising it to his lips he blows a mighty blast*)

The noise reverberates, hanging on the air until it becomes music. It grows louder, until suddenly we recognize Wagner's "The Ride of the Valkyries"

Filofax Look! (*He points to the sky, gaping, openmouthed*) Bloomin' heck! It's the SAS!
Svein The SAS?
Filofax Yeah! The Scandinavian Air Service!

The music swells

A great wind sweeps the stage, blowing Svein and Filofax and causing them to stagger. The howling wind rages against the swelling music until both reach a crescendo

> *Stuka, a magnificent figure in a winged helm, with regulation Luftwaffe goggles attached, and glittering silver armour, sweeps down from above to crash ignominiously on to the stage!*

Stuka *(raising the goggles)* Donner und Blitzen! Voss mit ze crazy music?
Svein I beg your pardon?
Stuka *(adjusting her metal breastplates)* Why heff you been summonink me mit ze horn of ze gotts, Schweinhund?
Svein Er ... I'm terribly sorry, but I don't understand. Who are you?
Stuka *(clicking her heels)* Oberst-Leutnant Stuka. At your service!
Svein Er ... Well, *what* are you?
Stuka Vott em I? Ich bin eine Walkyrie! Dumbkopf!
Filofax Blimey! A Valkyrie! Warlike female messenger of the gods!
Svein Gosh! Can you help us, Stuka? We are trapped in an invisible magic cell.
Stuka Can I help you? Gott in Himmel! Of course I can help you, dimvit! Vait vun minuten und I vill call down ze relentless barrage of powerful artillery fire!
Filofax Erm ... Don't you think that's a bit dangerous? I mean, mightn't we get hurt?
Stuka Nein! Absolutely unfichtnichtnig! Unthinkable! Ve Walkyrie are totally invincible!
Svein *(gently)* Yes, but we people aren't.
Stuka Ach! So! You are heffink a good point!
Filofax Can't you open the cell some other way?
Stuka Vott mit, Dumbkopf? You zink I am flyink around ze place mitt ze oxyacetylene gear?
Svein What about a counter-spell to release us? There must be one in the book!
Stuka Richtig! Let's heff a look! *(She leafs through the yellowing pages of the great book)* Mein Gott! Here it is! Now zen! Let me see ... *(She peers around suddenly)* Voss is das disgustink stench?
Svein Please hurry, our friends are in great danger, we must warn them!
Stuka Ja ja! Schnell, schnell! I'm goink as fast as I can! Here ve are... *(She reads from the book)*
"Unlock ze door, mit ze scent glands of skunk,
Allowink your prisoners to do a bunk."
Filofax Scent glands of skunk! So that's what the smell is!
Stuka *(rooting through the rows of jars)* Aha! Got it! Is zis it? *(She uncorks the jar and thrusts it towards the prisoners)*

Svein and Filofax both immediately keel over

(Nodding) Zat's it. *(She pours the contents of the bottle into the stone bowl)* Now zen ... *(She reads on)*
"You now heff ze key to open ze the cell,
So just add money to break ze spell!"

Act II Scene 1

Svein (*getting up and patting his pockets*) Money? (*To Filofax*) Have you got any money?
Filofax Nope.
Svein Why not?
Filofax (*accusingly*) When was the last time you paid me?
Svein Erm ... (*To Stuka*) Perhaps you could lend us some money?
Stuka Listen, Knucklekopf! I am a messenger of ze gotts! I am not flyink about ze shop mit ze pocketfuls of loose change! How vould I effer get off ze ground?
Svein (*agitated*) Well where can we get some money?
Filofax 'Ere! (*He nods at the audience*) What about asking this lot?
Svein Good idea! Stuka, could you ask to borrow some money from someone in the audience?
Stuka Jawohl!
Svein (*apprehensively*) Now ask nicely, won't you?
Stuka (*impatiently*) Ja ja! (*She turns to the audience*) ACHTUNG! You vill giff me all your money immediately, or you vill all be shot!
Svein Er, no ... That's not quite what I meant. Look, why don't you try the children. Use the children.
Stuka Ach! So! Goot idea! (*To the audience*) ACHTUNG! You vill giff me all your money immediately, or ve shoot ze children!
Svein No, no! Be nice! Ask the children politely, and I'm sure they'll help. Won't you, children?

Audience participation

Stuka Richtig! Got you! (*To the audience*) Achtung! Do you vish to release zese two idiots from ze magic cell?

Audience participation

Und do you vant to save Dame Dustbins und ze little Radisch from ze fate vorse zan death?

Enthusiastic audience participation

Und do you vish to see ze vicked Smug ze Smut defeated und humiliated?

Rapturous audience participation

Und do you vant to giff me all your money?

Nervous laughter from the audience

Svein (*tiredly*) We don't want all their money. Ten pence should do it
Stuka So! Wery Vell! Achtung children! HANDE HOCH! (*Apologetically*) Er ... I mean hends up: who voss cominck here today mit their mamas und papas?

A few children may put their hands up

So! Und who vould like to request their mamas und papas to lend zem ten pence, to lend to me to lend to ze two dumbkopf voss ist stucken in ze magic slammer? (*She selects a volunteer*)

The volunteer comes forward and hands over ten pence

Danke schon. Und now, ve vill effect ze jailbreak!

She adds the coin to the stone bowl, and there is another blinding flash. When the smoke clears, the imprisoning shaft of green light has vanished!

Filofax We're free! Free!
Svein (*shaking hands with Stuka*) How can I ever thank you enough?
Stuka Really, it's no problem. I am after all a far superior beink to you in every respect.
Filofax 'Cos you're an immortal?
Stuka (*puzzled*) No. because I am a voman.

Audience participation

Filofax Hey! The smell's gone!
Stuka (*peering into the bowl*) Und so has ze money!
Svein (*sternly*) Filofax.
Filofax (*innocently*) Hm?
Svein Hand it over.
Filofax (*mumbling*) It's not fair. I never get to keep any dosh.
Svein (*to the audience*) Whose is this ten pence?

The volunteer steps up

(*Giving the volunteer the coin und a bar of chocolate*) Here, thank you very much for your help. Have this bar of chocolate as well. I was going to give it to Filofax, but he doesn't deserve it now ... (*He turns to Stuka*) Tell me, how do we get to Troll Mountain from here?
Filofax I know! Why don't we hang on to her legs and she can fly us there?
Stuka Out of ze kvestion! Absolutely not! I can permit no fiddling mit my undercarriage.

Act II Scene 2

Filofax (*gloomily*) You sound like my wife.
Svein Well can you tell us how far away is it? One mile? Two? Three?
Stuka Nein.
Svein (*appalled*) Nine? Then we'll never make it!
Stuka Not nine, NEIN! It is ze mountain next to zis vun.
Svein Great! We may get there just in time then. Come on Filofax, let's go! Bye Stuka, and thanks again!

Filofax and Svein exit; the opening strains of "The Ride of the Valkyries" are heard again

Stuka No vorries Dumbkopf! I'll be seeink you! AUF WIEDERSEHEN!

She launches herself into mid-air and zooms off skyward

The Lights fade to Black-out

Scene 2

The Hall of Smut the Smug

Eric lounges on a bench noisily slurping Glögg from a trepanned skull. Thor scuffs on

Eric Wotcher. Want a skull of Glögg?
Thor (*gloomily*) No.
Eric What's up with you?
Thor I feel like a bad egg.
Eric Sorry, I'm fresh out of bad eggs. Have a Glögg.
Thor (*morosely*) Don't want any.
Eric You might as well — it tastes like bad eggs.
Thor (*snapping*) I don't want a Glögg!
Eric Suit yourself. Where's the boss?
Thor (*dismally*) He's gone up the mountain with a packed lunch for Stoneheart. We're supposed to follow him with Dame Dustpan.
Eric Oh. Well, she's still getting ready.
Thor (*uncomfortably*) Look, Eric. Couldn't we let her slip?
Eric Let her slip? Are you bonkers or what? We're already on half rations 'cos we let those kids escape! You heard what the boss said — another boob like that and we'll be for the high jump!
Thor So what? I'm sick of doing his dirty work! I think it's high time we stood up to him!
Eric (*incredulous*) Stood up to him? If we stood up to him, we'd never stand up again!

Thor Well, let's do a runner then!
Eric Have you ever tried running without kneecaps? (*He glances around*) Look out! She's coming.

Dame Dustpan enters

Er ... Hallo ... Enjoy your sauna then?
Dame (*distantly*) I feel like a steamed pudding.
Thor Strangely enough you look like one.
Eric Oh. Well, what about the plunge in the icy pool?
Dame I feel like a steamed pudding that has been shoved in the freezer ... (*She grabs Thor*) AND DON'T YOU DARE SAY I LOOK LIKE ONE! (*She slumps miserably*) Oh it's all too much! I shouldn't have to put up with this sort of thing at my time of life. (*She collapses in floods of tears*) Boo hoo hoo ...
Eric Oh great! That's all we need. Now look what you've done! Do something to cheer her up, will you?
Thor Er ... Right ... Here, Dame Dustpan, know what?
Dame (*snivelling*) What?
Thor Something really wonderful and exciting is happening today!
Dame (*brightening slightly*) Oh yes? What?
Thor You're getting married!
Dame (*caterwauling*) BOO HOO HOO HOO!
Eric (*drily*) Oh well done, Thor. You've really cheered her up now, haven't you!
Thor Well, I wasn't to know, was I? It's supposed to be the happiest day of a girl's life? Is it my fault she's not smitten with her intended?
Dame (*between sobs*) He's not my flamin' intended! He's my unintended! Boo hoo hoo!
Eric Oh for Pete's sake! Shut her up!
Thor I know! Why don't we sing her our jolly song! That'll cheer her up!
Eric Nar! She doesn't want to hear that.
Dame (*snuffling*) Oh yes I do!
Eric Eh?
Thor Yes! We can get all these people to help sing as well! (*To the audience*) You'll help us sing a jolly song to cheer up Dame Dustpan, won't you?

Audience participation

Right then! Who'd like to come up and join in?

Eric, Thor and Dame Dustpan descend into the audience to pressgang any poor unfortunates who don't sink quickly enough into their seats! Once the

Act II Scene 2

participants are lined up on stage, Eric commences his introduction, whilst handing out foam rubber cudgels to the children. (Twelve-inch lengths of foam pipe cladding should suffice)

Eric All right, here's what we're going to do. We're going to sing an old Viking bashing song. Basically, we all stand here and sing, and Thor ——
Thor (*cheerfully*) Hallo.
Eric — we bash him.
Thor (*alarmed*) Ere! Hang on a minute!
Eric So, as I was saying, I'll suggest a letter of the alphabet, you give me a part of Thor's body beginning with that letter — then we bash it. (*As an afterthought*) But we don't want anything naughty ...
Thor (*poking a few participants*) No! We *don't* want anything naughty, do we?
Eric Right, here we go then. Oh! I nearly forgot! You lot have to sing the chorus as well. It goes something like this. (*He sings the chorus, whilst absently thwacking Thor across the ear*)
        Bash, Bash, Bash, Bash, Bash, Bash, Bash,
        Bash, Bash, Bash, Bash, Bash, Bash, Bash!
There we are — got that? Not too complicated, I think you'll agree ... So, I'll start with the letter A. Who can give me a part of the body beginning with the letter A?

A number of suggestions are shouted by participants, and by the rest of the audience

(*Ignoring any* really *naughty words*) All right — Arm. That's a nice easy one to start with — Arm. I'll sing the verse, you all join in the chorus. Off we go then; when you're ready, maestro...

SONG 5
Bash! Bash! Bash!

Eric (*singing*)   I came across a Viking who was bashing up my home,
                        I took my club and bashed his ARM —
                        And this is how it goes!

During the chorus, Eric and Dame Dustpan encourage the children to thwack Thor about the arms with their rubber cudgels, whilst Thor cringes and complains

All   Bash! Bash! Bash! Bash! Bash! Bash! Bash!
               Bash! Bash! Bash! Bash! Bash! Bash! Bash!

Eric (*speaking*) There you go! That was fun, wasn't it?
Thor No.
Eric That wasn't at all bad, but don't forget to give Thor a good bashing, will you? Now then. Who can think of a part of the body beginning with the letter B?

... and so on, through as many letters of the alphabet as required, depending on the enthusiasm of the participants. After the first couple of times through, Dame Dustpan starts to join in the verse, visibly cheering up as the song progresses. The song should be concluded as follows:

Eric Well, just time for one last letter, I think. Let's have the letter K ... I know, why don't we ask Thor this time? Something beginning with the letter K, Thor?
Thor (*after brief consideration*) Kids.
Eric Kids?

Thor is passed a huge inflatable baseball bat from off stage

Thor (*emphatically*) Kids.
Eric Righto then.
　　(*Singing*) I came across a Viking who was bashing up my home,
　　　　I took my club and bashed his *KIDS*
　　And this is how it goes:

There is a final massed mêlée as all the children attempt to whack each other senseless, whilst Thor lays vengefully about him with his inflatable baseball bat!

All　　　　Bash! Bash! Bash! Bash! Bash! Bash! Bash!
　　　　　　Bash! Bash! Bash! Bash! Bash! Bash! Bash!
Eric Very good! Very good! Thank you very much indeed! A round of applause, ladies and gentlemen, please!

... and so on. Eric and Thor recover all the foam rubber cudgels, whilst Dame Dustpan hands out sweets to the participants, sampling a few herself at the same time. When all members of the audience have regained their seats, Thor turns solicitously to Dame Dustpan

Thor Feeling a bit better now?
Dame Oooh yes! Much better! I had no idea you dread Vikings could be such merry fellows!
Eric Oh well, we like to let our hair down now and then.

Act II Scene 2

Dame (*disarmingly*) Oh, I can see that.
Thor We know how to enjoy ourselves, all right.
Dame (*charming them*) You certainly do.
Eric We're no stick-in-the-muds!
Dame (*effusively*) Absolutely not!
Eric Er ... Yes, well ...
Dame (*happily*) Oh you're such good friends to me!
Eric Er ... Are we?
Dame Oh yes. The very best.
Eric (*nonplussed*) Oh.
Dame It's so important to have friends, don't you think? Friends you can *rely on in a crisis*?
Eric Er ... Oh yes ... yes ... very important.

There is a pregnant pause

Dame (*innocently*) Are we going up the mountain now?
Eric Um ...Well, yes, I suppose we'd better.
Thor (*outraged*) Hang on! We can't take her up there! She's our bestest friend!
Dame (*nobly*) No! No! I wouldn't dream of presuming on our friendship. You just drag me up that mountain and leave me in the brutal paws of a wicked Troll to spend the rest of me days in abject misery ——
Eric Now hang on a moment ——
Dame No! No! You go ahead. I wouldn't want you to land yourselves in trouble because of me. I know how to stand by me friends.
Eric Yes but ——
Dame No buts! I insist. (*Gallantly*) Deliver me to my grisly fate, my dear friends.
Eric No.
Thor (*surprised*) No?
Dame (*hopefully*) No?
Eric (*resolved*) No.
Dame What, you mean: "No-we're-not-going-up-the-mountain" *No*?
Eric Exactly.
Dame Oh. What a pity. Still, if you're sure I'll just collect me things and be on me way then.
Eric Wait!
Dame (*to the audience*) Blast! Nearly got away with it!
Eric Don't you think we should rescue Radish?
Dame Oh no. She'll be all right.
Thor What do you mean, "all right"? She's going to be eaten alive!
Dame (*hastily*) Yes, well, that's what I meant. She'll be all right to eat.

Eric (*thinking*) I mean, if we're going to do the dirty on the boss, we might as well do the job properly.

Dame Good idea! You go ahead, I'd only get in the way.

Eric (*his mind made up*) No. We need you to come with us. If we turn up without you, Smut may become suspicious, and we won't be able to save Radish from a fate worse than death!

Dame (*darkly*) Shame.

Eric (*sternly*) Dame Dustpan! What were you saying about standing by your friends?

Dame Oh yes. But I was planning to stand some way behind you, rather than actually *by* you...

Pause

Oh bother me boxer shorts! Out of the frying pan and into the bloomin' fire! Well, come on then, you Nordic nitwits! Let's get on with it!

They all turn to walk off

(*Artfully wheeling around to misquote heroically at the audience*) Once more down to the beach, dear friends, once more!

She is grabbed by Eric and Thor

(*Glowering*) And don't blame me if it gets too hot!

She is frogmarched off

The Lights fade to Black-out

Scene 3

The Hall of the Mountain King — Stoneheart's lair

This is a gloomy, subterranean chamber carved from the very rock of the mountain, littered with gruesome remains and decorated with grim, nightmarish banners. To one side, a stygian opening leads into a dark, winding passageway, where candles flicker eerily in the impenetrable blackness; there is a small doorway to the other side. A rope hangs down from one wall

Smut paces to and fro C

Smut (*ignoring any audience participation*) Come on, come on! Where have those blithering idiots got to? They should know better than to keep

Act II Scene 3

me waiting! Still, I won't have to put up with any of them much longer, will I? They'll all be blown to Valhalla soon enough! Ha ha ha!

Audience participation

Meanwhile Dame Dustpan, Eric and Thor enter through the small doorway to one side

At last! And where in Asgard have you been? (*With heavy sarcasm*) Admiring the scenery?
Dame (*surveying the set with a critical eye*) Blimey! You couldn't admire this scenery, could you?
Smut (*ignoring the interruption*) I don't pay you two clowns to dawdle around.
Thor (*muttering*) You don't pay us two clowns at all.
Smut What was that?
Eric (*hastily*) He said one of the clowns had a nasty fall.
Smut Hmmph. Well, you're here now, so we might as well get on with it ...
Dame (*interested*) Get on with what?
Smut With introducing you to your new husband, you repulsive old baggage! And providing him with his luncheon! Ha ha ha ha!

Audience participation

Smut crosses to the rope and tugs it. Tacky doorbell chimes play "La Cucaracha" or similar. A booming horn blast is heard together with the sound of a great stone slab rolling back somewhere below

(*Bellowing into the opening*) O Stoneheart! Lord of the Rock Trolls! King under the Mountain! I, Smut the Smug, Jarl of Shetland and Orkney, King of Dublin, Man and the Hebrides, Lord of the Isles, and Scourge of the Northern Seas, call upon thee to dine on the fruits which I, thy miserable servant, have laid before thee!

There is a sudden terrifying roar from below, and the sound of distant, monstrous footfalls approaching

Ha ha ha! He's on his way up! (*Shouting*) Bring on the smorgasbord!

Rollo trudges on, wheeling a large trolley, covered with a gleaming, domed silver lid

Excellent! Now, if you please, Rollo, let us inspect the bill of fare!

The lid is removed to reveal Radish trussed like a chicken on a giant salver.

She has an apple stuffed in her mouth, and is surrounded by piles of roast spuds and vegetables

Ha ha ha! And on the menu today, best end of Radish! Ha ha ha!

Audience participation

Dame (*spluttering*) Oh! You revolting, unspeakable barbarian!
Smut (*innocently*) Anything wrong?
Dame Yes! (*She points to the trolley*) You've overcooked the broccoli!

Another ferocious roar is heard, closer than before. The footsteps are getting louder. Radish starts to pull at her bonds

Smut Oh, Stoneheart isn't bothered by such culinary niceties! As long as the meat is fresh, he's usually happy. (*He prods Radish*)

Radish struggles more desperately

And you can't get much fresher than this, can you? Ha ha ha!

Audience participation

Suddenly, the footsteps cease. There is a momentary pause and then Stoneheart's amplified voice booms terrifyingly around the chamber

Stoneheart (*off*) Smut the Smug, is it?
Smut (*humbly*) Yes, your Immensity. It is I.
Stoneheart (*off*) My nosh you are bringing me, yes? My tribute?
Smut Er ... yes ... here it is, your Impressiveness! (*He produces a large knife*) Shall I carve?
Stoneheart (*off*) Wait!
Smut Certainly.
Stoneheart (*off, suspiciously*) What is to be carved?
Smut Er ... It's a human, my lord, your favourite; a girl, in fact ...
Stoneheart (*off, pondering*) Hummm ... Young and tender could it be?
Smut Oh, very young, your Balefulness, very tender.
Stoneheart (*off*) And succulent and juicy it is?
Smut Oh it is! She's ... er ... free range.
Stoneheart (*off*) Yum yum!
Smut And I have another little surprise for you, your Supremacy.
Stoneheart (*off*) Indeedy?
Smut Oh yes, indeedy.

Act II Scene 3

Stoneheart (*off*) What can it be that is so surprising? (*Hopefully*) Shiny gold is it? Or jewels perhaps? Precious metals?
Dame (*interrupting*) I think he probably means my humble self, your Beastliness.
Stoneheart (*off*) A humble self? What sort of surprising is this?
Smut (*hastily*) It is something to amuse you, your Immensity, a wife.
Stoneheart (*off*) A wifey? A lady troll?
Smut (*drily*) Well it almost certainly isn't human.
Stoneheart (*off*) Hideously ugly and horrendously coarse can it truly be?
Smut That about sums it up.
Stoneheart (*off*) Ho! Deep joy! A trollop for Stoneheart!
Dame Right! We'll soon put a stop to all this! (*She approaches the entrance*) Now listen here, boulder brain! If we're going to get hitched, there are going to have to be a few changes around here!
Stoneheart (*off*) Um?
Dame You may well "um", my little basalt bonce! I mean look at the state of this place! Cobwebs everywhere! And look at all these half-chewed bones lying around — it's like Saturday night outside the Kentucky Fried Chicken shop!
Smut (*calling solicitously*) I'm afraid she's not very polite. Would you rather I simply bashed her head in?
Stoneheart (*off*) No no! Deliciously rude and obnoxious she is sounding! A perfect match!
Dame Oh, Gawd.
Smut Er... Well... Fine. I must be going now, I have important business to attend to down the mountain.
Stoneheart (*off*) Of course. Quite understanding I am.
Smut Oh. Right then... Well... Your meal awaits you... er... bon appetit! (*To Eric and Thor*) You two numbskulls stay here and make sure they don't escape!
Thor Stay here? With his lordship on his way up? Not flamin' likely!
Eric (*hissing*) Shut up, you idiot! (*To Smut*) Actually we'd love to stay here and guard the prisoners, boss! Wouldn't we, Thor? (*He nudges him*)
Thor Would we?
Eric Yes. 'Cos if we're guarding them they won't be able to *escape*, will they?
Thor Won't they? (*The penny dropping*) Oh right! No! Of course they won't!
Smut That's better! Well... (*He smiles slyly*) I'll see you later I expect. Come Rollo, we have work to do. Ha ha ha!

Smut and Rollo exit to audience participation

Dame (*as soon as they are gone*) Right! Don't just stand there! Help me get her out of this! (*She starts to free Radish*)
Stoneheart (*off*) Ready for din-dins now! Coming up, I am...

The sound of huge, heavy footsteps grows louder

Eric Oh no! He's coming! What are we going to do?
Thor (*shouting*) Hit the panic button!
Dame Wait a minute! Wait a minute! Whatever you do, don't panic! (*She yells desperately into the hole*) 'Ere. Have you washed yer paws?
Stoneheart (*off*) Um?
Dame You have to wash your hands before you sit down to eat. (*To the audience*) Don't you, boys and girls?

Audience participation

(*Ignoring those that shout "No!"*) See?
Stoneheart (*off; whining*) Oh. Do I have to?
Dame Yes you jolly well do! You mucky troll!
Stoneheart (*off*) Huh ... Oh, very well ...
Dame Thank Gawd for that! Right, come on. (*They succeed in freeing Radish*) Now let's get out of here ... (*She tries the door*) Bloomin' heck! It's locked! Old Hagar the Horrible locked us in!
Stoneheart (*off*) Washed my hands I have. Coming up now.
Eric Oh no? What are we going to do now?
Stoneheart (*off*) Here I'm coming, ready or not!
Radish Remember, whatever you do, don't panic.
Dame What do you mean, don't panic? He only wants to *eat* you! I've got to marry him! I dread to think what he wants from his "Wifey"!
Eric Right then. So we're agreed. Thor?
Thor (*obliging*) Panic!

All four rush around, scrambling desperately to get furthest away from the entrance as the footsteps get louder and louder until they are reverberating round the chamber ...

> *... and suddenly, there in the entrance stands a diminutive old gentleman wearing a long white beard and an immense pair of boots, clutching a megaphone in one hand. This is Santa Claus*

Santa Hallo.

The others stare at him in stupefied silence

Act II Scene 3

Er ... (*He speaks through the megaphone*) FEE FIE FOE FUM?
Dame (*gobsmacked*) You're Stoneheart?
Santa Er ... well, yes, I suppose I am really.
Radish (*emerging from hiding*) But you're the little old man who lives around the mountain!
Santa Well, strictly speaking, I'm the little old man who lives on top of the mountain.
Radish But you don't eat people ... surely?
Santa Oh, good Lord no, that's just a ploy to scare away the visitors.
Radish So what happens to all the children Smut sends up here to be devoured by the troll?
Santa Oh, you know, they help me in my workshops for a while and then I send them home.
Dame (*realization dawning*) Wait a mo! I know you ...
Radish Your workshops?
Santa Where the toys are made.
Dame (*incredulously*) Blimey! It can't be!
Santa (*rather embarrassed*) I'm afraid it is. (*He pats his stomach*) Ho ho ho!
Dame Blimey O'Reilly! (*To Radish*) It's dear old Santa!
Radish (*to Thor*) Santa Claus!
Thor (*to Eric*) Santa Claus!
Eric (*to no-one in particular*) Santa Claus! (*He looks at the others*) Wait a minute! I don't believe in Santa Claus!
Dame 'Ere! What's happened to me wards, then?
Santa Why they're here of course! (*Calling into the tunnel*) Come along, children!

Tum, Dickon and Harald bowl out of the entrance and run to Dame Dustpan, laughing and shouting

Dame (*fending them off*) All right! All right! Blimey! And I was hopin' you three'd been scoffed by a troll. No such luck, eh?
Radish If you're Santa Claus, why do you put up with Smut the Smug? He is cruel and despicable!
Santa I know, my dear. But there are advantages to having a villainous brute as a gatekeeper; he keeps away unwanted visitors. Poor Smut. He hasn't a clue about my real identity.
Dame 'Ere! I say, Sant — did you get the letter I sent you last Christmas?
Santa Of course.
Dame Oh. Well why didn't I get ——
Santa (*interrupting*) Dame Dustpan. I make toys, not surgical appliances.

The children roar with laughter

Suddenly the door bursts open and Svein and Filofax tumble in

Dame Well well! It's the dynamic duo! Better late than never, I suppose ... Where have you been?
Filofax (*conspiratorially*) We have ... intelligence ...
Dame You could have fooled me.
Svein Where is Stoneheart? (*He peers at Santa*) Is this one of your boyfriends?
Dame Cheek! This is Santa Claus! Stoneheart was just a cover!
Svein Crikey! Well, where's Smut?
Dame He left, and good riddance to bad rubbish!
Svein Then there is no time to lose! Smut plans to blow this hall sky high, with all of you in it!
Dame Oooh! The sneaky beaky!
Santa (*anxiously*) We must stop him! He will flatten my workshop! All the toys for Christmas will be destroyed!
Dame But we'll never catch him in time! He'll be halfway down the mountain by now!
Svein (*inspired*) Toboggan!
Dame Well really! There's no call for that sort of language!
Svein I've got it! We'll use Santa's sleigh! We'll ski down the mountain!
Dame Ooooh, skiing! How exciting! (*To the audience*) I've never been on the piste, you know!
Filofax (*aside*) That's not what I've heard.
Svein Come on! We must hurry! (*He catches sight of Radish*) Radish!
Radish Svein!
Svein (*remembering he is a prince*) Er ... Hallo.
Radish (*shyly*) Hallo.
Dame (*barging between them*) 'ALLO! Do I smell the sickly sweet scent of romance in the air? Come on, no time for any lovey-dovey nonsense! You said we had to hurry!
Svein Yes but ... (*He drags his gaze away from Radish*) Oh very well. Come on then! Let's do it!
Dame (*leering*) Oooh yes: let's!
All HURRAY!

SONG 6
Dame, Svein, Filofax, Santa, Radish, Eric, Thor, Tum, Dickon and Harald

All exit

The Lights fade to Black-out

Smut's Saga

Scene 4

The Hall of Smut the Smug

Smut and Rollo enter, unwinding a drum of explosive fuse

Smut (*irritably*) Come on, Come on! We haven't got all day. I'm going to fix Stoneheart once and for all! And then I'll be King under the mountain, and all the other morons will have to pay me tribute! Ha ha ha ha! (*He pauses and sniffs*) What's that revolting smell?

Horrible Helga staggers on under the weight of a detonator box with a plunger protruding from the top

Helga Coooeee! Hallo Smutty me old mucker. You big hunk of Danish Blue you! Har har har!
Smut (*grunting*) Oh. It's you. Well? I've laid the gunpowder charges. How do I set them off?
Helga (*referring to the detonator*) With this ...
Smut Right. Give it here.
Helga (*slyly*) Actually Smut, I've been thinkin' ...
Smut Oh yes?
Helga Yes. I've been thinkin' p'r'aps you and I should get together — you know, work a bit more closely, if you take my meaning ...
Smut All right. I'll think about it. Give me the detonator...
Helga (*persistently*) No, I mean work a bit more *closely*. I mean to say, a Viking in your position ought to have a proper home to come back to after a hard day's murderin', not to mention someone fluffy for a bit of snuggle-pie! Har har har!
Smut Snuggle-pie! What, you and me? You've got to be kidding!
Helga Eh?
Smut A handsome brute like me take up with a scaly old hag like you? Ha ha ha ha! What would I want with you? I'm such a magnificent beast I could have beautiful girls by the dozen! (*Appealing to the audience*) Couldn't I?

Audience participation

Bah! Shut up! (*To Helga*) Anyway, just hand over the detonator before I chop your scabby ears off!
Helga (*outraged*) How dare you! Well! I was goin' to tell you something very interestin' but now I shan't! So there!
Smut What?

Helga No, no. Nothin'. Doesn't matt——

Smut seizes Helga by the throat

——aaaark!

Smut Now listen here, you festering old scragbag. If you don't want to be bashed from here to Greenland, you'd better tell me what you're talking about!

Helga (*shrieking*) Let me go! Let me go! You'll be sorry! I'll put a spell on you!

Smut (*shaking her*) Oh yeah? Listen you ugly old crow! By the time I've finished with you, the only thing you'll be putting on is a plaster cast! So spill the beans — or else!

Helga (*choking*) All right! All right! Put me down! I'll tell you. (*She gulps for air*) I've got Svein Goldenhair and the dwarf banged up at my place. They were on their way to pay you a visit.

Smut (*dropping Helga in the dirt*) Hmmmm ... were they? Well, I'll deal with them later. Meanwhile, I've got more important fish to fry. Rollo! Throw this hideous old slag into the fjord. She could do with a wash.

Rollo drags Helga towards the exit; Smut relieves her of the detonator

I'll take that.

Helga (*spitting with venom as she is hauled across the floor*) I'll get you for this, you great fat oaf, you just see if I don't.

Smut (*calmly*) Goodbye Helga. Thank you so much for dropping in.

Rollo and Helga exit

Ha ha ha ha! Now I've got this, my devious plan is almost complete! No more Stoneheart! No more Radish! No more Dame Dustpan! Ha ha! And then I'll deal with Svein the vain. How does that sound, eh?

Audience participation

Ha ha ha ha! Too bad, suckers! Looks like the good guys have lost this time! (*He connects up the detonator and the fuse*) Now then, how does this go ... ?

A faint screaming is heard in the distance

(*Peering around*) What in Valhalla is that?

The screaming rapidly grows louder

Act II Scene 4

What's going on, by Odin?

Words are now discernible in the screaming: "I want to get off!", "Help! We're going to crash!", "How do you steer this thing?" etc

There is a sudden, rending crash as a huge sleigh smashes straight through the wall of Smut's hall, ripping open an enormous hole and flinging snow and debris everywhere! The dazed passengers — Dame, Svein, Filofax, Santa, Radish, Eric, Thor, Tum, Dickon and Harald — tumble off

Smut stares in utter disbelief

Dame *(reeling through the gaping hole in the wall)* These modern buildings you know ... The walls are just paper-thin ...
Smut *(raging)* WHAT HAVE YOU DONE TO MY HALL?
Svein *(getting unsteadily to his feet)* Smut the Smug! I want a word with you!
Smut *(amazed)* You? But I thought you ——
Radish *(pushing past Svein)* Well, you thought wrong!
Smut And you! But how did you escape? What happened to Stoneheart? Is he off his food?
Dame Never mind all that! Prepare to receive your up-commance!
Smut Oho! In that case I shall first put paid to the Hall of the Mountain King! *(He moves to depress the plunger on the detonator)*
Santa *(shouting)* NO! Don't touch that! You'll destroy my workshops!
Smut *(puzzled)* What workshops? Who is this old gnome? *(He peers at Dame Dustpan)* Is this your boyfriend?
Dame *(irately)* No, it flamin' well isn't!
Smut Well you'd better listen to him whoever he is, otherwise there's going to be a very big bang, and the top of Troll Mountain will be shorter by about a hundred foot!
Svein You are a coward, Smut! Have you forgotten what it is to be a Viking? Do not hide behind your tricks, rather let us test our steel in heroic combat!
Smut Heroic combat? No chance! I'm not stupid! Now clear off, before I start the fireworks!
Santa *(to Svein)* Please! Don't provoke him! *(To Smut)* I implore you, sir, not to do anything hasty!
Svein *(reluctantly)* Very well. What if we leave you alone? What guarantee do we have that you won't set off an explosion anyway?
Smut *(grandiosely)* You have my word of honour as a pirate and a bandit.
Svein *(grimly)* Hardly very reassuring.
Smut Take it or leave it. Ha ha ha!
Filofax Hey! Isn't this a moment of direst danger?
Smut Eh?
Filofax *(to the audience)* What do you think folks? Is this another moment of direst danger?

Audience participation

Svein Of course! The horn! (*He pulls out the horn*)
Smut 'Ere! What's going on?
Dame Yes, what's going on?

Svein blows a mighty blast upon the horn, and the strains of Wagner are immediately heard in the distance

Ooooh! Culture! Oh I do love a bit of the old classical music, girls. Mozart, Brahms and Liszt; that spotty git with the violin ...
Smut (*raising the detonator over his head*) I'm warning you! Any tricks and I'll blow the whole place sky high!
Svein (*stepping forward*) All right, Smut. The game's up. Come on, hand it over——
Smut Never! Get back! I'm warning you!

The music rises to a crescendo

Stuka swoops down from above and swipes the detonator from Smut's hands

What the ...?
Dame Bloomin' heck! It's Dumbo!
Filofax We appear to have gained air supremacy.
Stuka (*landing beside Svein*) Is zis vot you vanted?
Svein It is. Thank you.
Stuka No vorries. You like me to sort out zis dumbkopf?
Svein I think we can deal with him now.
Stuka Okey doke.
Smut (*snarling*) Oh, you think you can handle me, do you? Well well well! The question is, can you handle the strongest warrior in all Smutland? Ha ha ha!
Svein What?
Smut (*yelling*) ROLLO!
Svein Ooer! I forgot about him.
Stuka (*with interest*) Who ist Rollo?
Eric He's Smut's minder.
Thor A giant.
Eric Brain the size of a pea——
Thor —but with the strength of ten men.
Eric (*knowledgeably*) He's a Berserk.
Dame Never mind Berserk, pal, he's stark raving bonkers!

Act II Scene 4   55

Smut Ha ha ha! Indeed! Prepare to be pulverized! (*Bellowing*) ROLLO!

A figure appears in the doorway, but it is not Big Rollo. Drenched and covered in seaweed, the figure sloshes into the room, a puddle forming at its feet. It is Helga

Helga Hallo, Smut.
Smut You? Where is Rollo?
Helga We took a tumble into the fjord! Luckily I remembered I had my magic wand with me! I turned him into a herring! (*She produces a fish and holds it under Smut's nose*) Would you like my last Rollo? Har har har!
Smut (*horrified*) No!
Helga (*hissing*) Yes! You treacherous, double-dealing viper! I've got a score to settle with you!
Smut (*in terror*) No!
All YES!
Radish Go on! Turn him into something!
Helga I intend to! Any requests?

Eric and Thor put their hands up and jump up and down

Radish Santa?
Smut Santa? Where did he spring from?
Santa Ho hum. Yes, well ... as I shall be losing my young helpers, and Smut won't be supplying me with any more. I could use some assistance in my workshops ...
Smut (*backing away*) No ... No you wouldn't.
All OH YES WE WOULD!
Helga Easily done!

All the Lights, save a spot on Helga, fade during the following verse

    Abracadabra — a spell off the shelf
    Will transform the Viking into an elf!
 SHAZZAM! (*She flourishes her wand and flings a handful of glitter*)

There is a Black-out and a brilliant flash. The Lights come up on smoke: as this clears, Smut the Smug is revealed, transformed. He now wears a pointy red hat, green pointy shoes, and large pointy rubber ears! When he speaks, his voice is a high-pitched warble

Smut (*gurgling*) Oh no! What have you done?
Dame Blimey! It's Santa's little helper!

Smut I don't feel very well.
Dame You look Elfy enough. (*To the audience*) Elfy! Geddit? Oh, never mind.

Snorri Snorrisson enters

Snorri Santa! There you are!
Santa Ah, Snorri my old friend, I'd like you to meet my new assistant ...
Snorri Ah! An elf. How do you do.
Smut (*depressed*) Oh, great.
Snorri And Prince Svein: how goes your quest, your highness? Have you found a princess to banish the snows from the summer country?
Svein Good sir, I think I have found my true love, but she is no princess. (*He shyly takes hands with Radish*) My lands, alas, must remain in the Frost King's icy grip.
Snorri But what of the Princess Meadowsweet?
Svein (*looking down*) Of her I have found no sign.
Snorri Have you not? (*He smiles indulgently*) Oh Svein — sometimes we look so hard for the trees, we cannot see the wood. Open your eyes, my Prince, and follow your heart.
Svein What do you mean?
Radish (*lost in a trance*) Meadowsweet ... I have a distant memory of such a name. As I lay in my mother's arms, before I was taken ...
Svein (*in amazement*) Radish? (*He grabs Dame Dustpan by the arm*) Could this be her?
Dame Well! I don't know, let me see ——
Svein (*shouting*) Could it?
Dame How should I know? She was a baby last time I saw her and babies all look alike, don't they, all dribble and stickiness whichever end you look at them.
Svein (*tightly*) Just answer.
Dame (*flustered*) All right! Yes! Probably. I 'spect ...
Svein (*fervently embracing Radish*) Oh Radish!
Radish Oh Svein!
Svein (*overcome*) Oh Meadowsweet!
Filofax Oh Cowpat!
Dame Oh Gawd blimey!
Smut Oh cut it out! We haven't got all night!
Santa Quite so. Come along, elf. We've got work to do.
Dame Oooh yes! You will be able to get all the toys made by Christmas, won't you?
Santa I hope so, now I have an assistant to share the burden.

Act II Scene 4   57

Dame Oooh well, don't overwork him, will you? After all, we don't want your Elf to suffer! (*To the audience*) Elf to suffer, geddit? That's another elf joke! Oh, suit yourselves ...
Svein I know! We'll all help you! That way, you'll be sure to have everything ready by the night before Christmas!
Santa Oh I say everybody! Would you?
All YES!
Radish (*throwing her arms around Svein*) And we shall be wed on Christmas morning!
Snorri In that case, I shall throw a grand Christmas wedding party, a great feast of celebration.
All HURRAY!
Snorri At which I shall tell some more sagas ——
All NOOOOOOOO!
Snorri (*with a sniff*) Philistines!

Festive music. The whole cast assembles on stage for the Grand Finale

Snorri	And so my friends, our saga ends.
	I hope we have not bored you.
Santa	You have seen how good will always win
	If your hero stays valiant and true!
Svein	I have learned that things aren't always
	Exactly as they seem.
Radish	I have found my freedom, and true love,
	(*Mistily*) It's like a magic dream!
Filofax	YUCK!
Tum	We've learned to be good not naughty,
Dickon	No more "E" numbers or preservatives
Harald	And when we get home to England
	We're joining the Young Conservatives!

Eric (*whispering desperately to Thor*) The old trout only wants me to marry her ——
Thor (*dubiously*) That's rather a lot to take on ——
Dame (*sliding a brawny arm around Eric*)
 He may not have "Danish" stamped on his bum,
 But we'll soon be making bacon!
Smut (*pushing his way to the front*)
 I used to be a terrifying villain,
 I even frightened myself,
 But now I'm lumbered with Santa's chores,
 Proving villainy's bad for your Elf!

Santa	Enjoy yourselves this Christmas time
	With lots of festive cheer
Dame (*steering Santa towards the exit*)
	But now Santa's taking me to the pub
	To buy me a lots of beer!
	So, night night, and
All	MERRY CHRISTMAS!

SONG 7
All

CURTAIN

FURNITURE AND PROPERTY LIST

ACT I

Scene 1

On stage: Huge book for **Snorri**
Long table
Benches
Furs
Chain

Scene 2

On stage: Oars for **Oarsmen**
Bleached skull for **Smut**

Personal: **Smut**: axe

Scene 3

Off stage: Broom (**Dame Dustpan**)

Scene 4

Off stage: Sack (**Eric and Thor**)

Personal: **Eric and Thor**: swords
Eric: large war axe

Scene 5

Off stage: Sword, rubber cudgel (**Rollo**)
Iron collars, chain (**Tum, Dickon and Harald**)
Fur-wrapped parcel. *In it*: horn (**Snorri**)

Personal: **Smut**: diary

Scene 6

On stage: Booty on ship

ACT II

Scene 1

On stage: Book for **Snorri**
Crude timber furniture
Bottled potions
Ancient, dusty books
Jars containing weird flora and fauna
Barrel with skull and crossbones on it
Empty gin bottles
Mound of filthy, ragged clothing
Small stone bowl

Personal: **Svein**: horn, bar of chocolate

Scene 2

On stage: Trepanned skull for **Eric**

Off stage: Foam rubber cudgels (**Eric** and **Thor**)
Huge inflatable baseball bat (**Thor**)

Personal: **Dame Dustpan**: sweets

Scene 3

On stage: Gruesome remains
Rope

Off stage: Large trolley covered with domed silver lid. *Under lid*: roast potatoes, vegetables (**Rollo**)

Scene 4

Off stage: Drum of explosive fuse (**Smut** and **Rollo**)
Detonator box (**Helga**)

Personal: **Svein**: horn
Helga: handful of glitter, fish, wand

LIGHTING PLOT

Property fittings required: candles in ACT II, SCENE 3

Various interior and exterior settings

ACT I, SCENE 1

To open: Darkness

Cue 1	Low throb of ominous music *Bring up single spotlight* C	(Page 1)
Cue 2	Knock on gate, fading away *Bring up full interior lights slowly*	(Page 2)
Cue 3	**Snorri**: "Sailing for England ... " *Fade to black-out*	(Page 4)

ACT I, SCENE 2

To open: Darkness

Cue 4	Drumbeat, growing louder *Bring up weird, shifting light*	(Page 4)
Cue 5	**Oarsmen** resume chanting *Lights dim*	(Page 6)
Cue 6	Longship moves into mist *Black-out*	(Page 6)

ACT I, SCENE 3

To open: General exterior lighting

Cue 7	**Dame**: " ... they called it the Dark Ages?" *Black-out*	(Page 9)
Cue 8	**Dame**: "And it lasts for ages ... " *Bring up full lights*	(Page 9)
Cue 9	**Dame Dustpan** exits *Fade lights to black-out*	(Page 10)

ACT I, Scene 4

To open: General exterior lighting

| Cue 10 | **Eric** and **Thor** exit
Black-out | (Page 14) |

ACT I, Scene 5

To open: General exterior lighting

| Cue 11 | **Dame**, **Svein** and **Filofax** exit
Black-out | (Page 21) |

ACT I, Scene 6

To open: General exterior lighting

| Cue 12 | End of Song 4
Black-out | (Page 29) |

ACT II

ACT II, Scene 1

To open: Darkness

| Cue 13 | When ready
Solo spot on **Snorri** | (Page 30) |

| Cue 14 | **Snorri**: "Where is Prince Svein the Fair?"
Bring up light on **Svein** *and* **Filofax** | (Page 30) |

| Cue 15 | **Snorri**: "... devious sorceress."
Cross-fade spot on **Snorri** *to interior lights on* **Helga**'s *cave* | (Page 31) |

| Cue 16 | **Helga**: "... a spell of power!"
Black-out, then bring up shaft of green light | (Page 34) |

| Cue 17 | Flash from flashbox
Cut shaft of green light | (Page 38) |

Smut's Saga

Cue 18	**Stuka** zooms off skyward *Fade lights to black-out*	(Page 39)

ACT II, Scene 2

To open: General interior lighting

Cue 19	**Eric, Thor** and **Dame Dustpan** exit *Fade lights to black-out*	(Page 44)

ACT II, SCENE 3

To open: Gloomy interior lighting; flickering candle effect in passageway

Cue 20	**All** exit *Fade lights to black-out*	(Page 51)

ACT II, Scene 4

To open: General interior lighting

Cue 21	**Helga**: "Easily done!" *Fade general lights; bring up spot on* **Helga**	(Page 55)
Cue 22	**Helga** flings a handful of glitter *Black-out*	(Page 55)
Cue 23	Flash from flash box; smoke *Bring up general lights*	(Page 55)

EFFECTS PLOT

ACT I

Cue 1	**When ready** *Low throb of ominous music*	(Page 1)
Cue 2	**Snorri:** "Olaf Shipbuilder, Olaf ... " *Mighty knock on gate; sound reverberates, then fades away*	(Page 1)
Cue 3	**Lights come up on Snorri's hall** *More knocking*	(Page 2)
Cue 4	**Snorri pulls the chain** *Sound of great timber gates creaking open*	(Page 2)
Cue 5	**At beginning of Scene 2** *Sound of heavy seas and gusting winds; drumbeat, growing louder; fog effect*	(Page 4)
Cue 6	**At beginning of Scene 3** *Mist effect*	(Page 6)
Cue 7	**Rollo:** "Don't be so flamin' cheeky!" *Flash and bang*	(Page 15)
Cue 8	**Snorri:** "May good fortune accompany your quest!" *Flash and bang*	(Page 17)
Cue 9	**Dame Dustpan wafts her skirts** *Loud raspberry*	(Page 27)

ACT II

Cue 10	**Svein:** "But where is Horrible Helga?" *Sinister music*	(Page 32)
Cue 11	**Helga:** "... a spell of power!" *Flash, then smoke*	(Page 34)
Cue 12	**Svein blows the horn** *Horn sound reverberates and becomes music — "The Ride of the Valkyries"*	(Page 35)

Smut's Saga

Cue 13	**Filofax:** "The Scandinavian Air Service!" *Music swells; wind sound comes in; wind and music reach a crescendo together*	(Page 35)
Cue 14	**Stuka** adds the coin to the bowl *Flash and smoke*	(Page 38)
Cue 15	**Filofax** and **Svein** exit *Opening strains of "The Ride of the Valkyries"*	(Page 39)
Cue 16	**Smut** tugs the rope *Tacky doorbell chimes playing "La Cucaracha"; then a booming horn blast and sound of a great stone slab rolling back*	(Page 45)
Cue 17	**Smut:** "... have laid before thee!" *Terrifying roar and distant, monstrous footfalls approaching; continue footsteps under dialogue*	(Page 45)
Cue 18	**Dame:** "You've overcooked the broccoli!" *Ferocious roar; footsteps become progressively louder under following dialogue*	(Page 46)
Cue 19	**Stoneheart:** (*off*) "Coming up, I am ... " *Footsteps become even louder*	(Page 48)
Cue 20	**Thor:** "Panic!" *Footsteps become even louder*	(Page 48)
Cue 21	Sleigh crashes through wall *Rending crash*	(Page 53)
Cue 22	**Svein** blows the horn *Strains of Wagner in the distance*	(Page 54)
Cue 23	**Smut:** "I'm warning you." *Music rises to a crescendo*	(Page 54)
Cue 24	**Helga** flings a handful of glitter *Flash; smoke*	(Page 55)
Cue 25	**Snorri:** "Philistines!" *Festive music*	(Page 57)

The notice printed below on behalf of the Performing Right Society should be carefully read if any other copyright music is used in this play.

The permission of the owner of the performing rights in copyright music must be obtained before any public performance may be given, whether in conjunction with a play or sketch or otherwise, and this permission is just as necessary for amateur performances as for professional. The majority of copyright musical works (other than oratorios, musical plays and similar dramatico-musical works) are controlled in the British Commonwealth by the PERFORMING RIGHT SOCIETY LTD, 29-33 Berners Street, London W1P 4AA.

The Society's practice is to issue licences authorizing the use of its repertoire to the proprietors of premises at which music is publicly performed, or, alternatively, to the organizers of musical entertainments, but the Society does not require payment of fees by performers as such. Producers or promoters of plays, sketches, etc., at which music is to be performed, during or after the play or sketch, should ascertain whether the premises at which their performances are to be given are covered by a licence issued by the Society, and if they are not, should make application to the Society for particulars as to the fee payable.

A separate and additional licence from PHONOGRAPHIC PERFORMANCES LTD, Ganton House, Ganton Street, London W1, is needed whenever commercial recordings are used.

A NOTE ON CHARACTERIZATION

Snorri Snorrisson is a bard and saga maker. The Viking term is "Skald" — but as you will see, Snorri is not too hot. Nonetheless, he fulfills a vital role in introducing the saga, and even manages to intrude upon the action once or twice! His costume should consist of sagely robes, long white hair and a matching beard. This role offers considerable scope for would-be hams, although it can be played absolutely straight to good effect.

Smut the Smug is a departure from the sibilant, evil school of traditional pantomime villainy. He is a brutish creature, violent and uncouth. His unconcealed lust for power and wealth is matched by a foul temper and childish malevolence. He is used to getting his own way, and cannot tolerate dissent. He relies on his giant sidekick for his strength, and whilst adept at terrorizing the old and the weak, he is revealed as a coward in the face of a challenge from Svein. Smut cannot be played for laughs, but must be portrayed as a coarse, swaggering bully in studs and black leather, the boss of the tenth-century equivalent of a motorcycle gang.

Big Rollo has little to say, but makes a big impact as he is about nine feet tall! This is easily accomplished by sitting one actor upon the shoulders of another, and garbing the pair in a robe of matted fur fabric reaching down to below the knees of the lower half! The upper half is fitted out with a broad padded chest, and a pair of extended arms encased in long sleeves, terminating in gauntleted false hands. The head may look a little on the small side, but this can be overcome with the addition of a large wig, helmet and false beard! Needless to say, the two halves of Rollo must practice a good deal to achieve a comfortable (and safe) synergy — but the result can appear surprisingly effective.

Dame Dustpan is an indomitable figure, capable of outright belligerence and cringing cowardice almost simultaneously! She is coarse, lewd and rather vain, but exhibits redeeming pantomime dame qualities of endurance and adaptability — as well as a suitably appalling line in groanworthy jokes.

Tum, Dickon and **Harald** are nominally boys, but their gender is frankly immaterial. They present a noisy and irreverent challenge to the authority of the adult world, oblivious to whether their victim is friend or foe! They should be unashamedly abusive towards their elders and betters. Kids in the audience are sure to identify with such heroics.

Eric and **Thor** fulfil the traditional role of brokers' men. According to convention, one should be tall and thin, one short and fat. Eric is completely stupid, but he's an intellectual giant compared to Thor! The latter does possess a heart of gold, however, and it is he who persuades Eric to defect from Smut's employ, allowing the two Vikings to line up with the goodies come the curtain call!

Svein, Prince of the Blue Fjords should be tall, dashing and good-looking, as befits a principal boy. His costume should be martial and richly decorated. As a Viking Prince, Svein should ideally be blond, but this is not essential. You can always change his name to Svein the Fair, *Raven* Hair.

Filofax is a typical dwarf, surly, cynical and insubordinate. He tries to be a good servant, but his loyalty to his master is sometimes transcended by his own highly developed instinct for self-preservation. Filofax should nonetheless present a sturdy and formidable figure in leathern jerkin and hooded cloak.

Radish is slender, brave and delectable. She is subjected to a catalogue of cruel indignities by Smut, but rises above all degradation with a spirit and resourcefulness which betrays her true lineage. Her costume should be fetchingly threadbare allowing her natural radiance to shine through.

Helga Forkbeard is a revolting harridan, completely mad but possessed of a certain native cunning. Her costume should be outlandish, her make-up weird, and her acting blatantly over-the-top!

Stuka the Valkyrie is a supernatural being of immense power from Nordic myth. In our story, she is a benign influence, but only just ...

Stoneheart. Now Stoneheart never actually appears because he doesn't really exist. (He is, in fact, Santa's alter-ego.) His characterization, therefore, is wholly dependent on voice, which should be redolent with menace, fearsomely amplified, and (where technical facilities permit) generously loaded with echo. A word of warning: it's safer to speak the role live with a microphone, than to rely on all the other characters interacting with a pre-recorded voice.

Santa Claus. What can I say? He's got to be fat, he's got to be jolly, he's got to wear a fur-lined red anorak.

Vikings. You can have as many of these as you like, in all shapes and sizes to use up any available supernumeraries. It's amazing how even the pinkest child can attain a highly disreputable aspect with the aid of a false beard, a layer of Leichner dirt, and a barbaric outfit liberally concocted from fur fabric and imitation leather! Although the chorus isn't written into the action very much, they can be deployed in several places, especially in Smut's scenes, where they can usefully prod prisoners along, or lug sacks of booty about.

(Incidentally, for the record, Vikings didn't wear horned helmets. In Norse mythology, that prerogative was reserved for the gods. However, this is pantomime ...)

PRODUCTION NOTES

As with most pantomimes, stage settings for *Smut's Saga* can be as rudimentary or sophisticated as budget, time and ingenuity will allow.

In the original production, settings were deliberately understated for the most part — but spiced up by very high-impact treatment of a few key scenes and effects! Only one full backdrop was employed (to depict the dramatic fjordland mountainscape of ACT I Scene 6). Otherwise settings were suggested by judicious use of stage properties, furniture and stand-alone sections of scenery, deployed in front of a plain black backcloth and legs.

Amateur pantomimes often benefit from this sort of minimalist approach. It's usually better to focus creative effort on the construction and painting of a few key items, well made and lovingly painted, rather than turning out masses of crudely daubed, slapdash scenery.

The script allows for entrances stage left and right and also through the audience on to a raised forestage area, where parts of the action taking place in front of the main curtains can be played out whilst scenes are changed behind.

EFFECTS

A number of effects are called for during the course of the play. These may at first appear slightly daunting, but are in fact relatively straightforward to achieve and should certainly not deter anyone from staging the show! It may however be helpful to prospective directors to know how these effects were accomplished in our original production. This information is offered by way of general guidance only; what works well in one venue may not necessarily be viable in another. You will probably wish to develop your own methods of achieving the desired effects.

The Ride of the Valkyries

Only the largest theatres are likely to be equipped with flying facilities, and whilst this equipment can be hired, it will make a hefty dent in your production budget.

In the original production, Stuka the Valkyrie abseiled down on to the stage in brisk SAS fashion. This wasn't really flying, but it certainly achieved the desired dramatic effect!

Clearly, this option is dependent firstly on access to sufficient overhead space above the stage, and secondly on the actress portraying Stuka being agile (and intrepid) enough to tackle the abseiling! If you decide to employ this method, try to borrow the necessary equipment from your local climbing club or boy scouts. They'll probably be willing to give some tuition as well.

Make sure that there is a stable overhead platform (with handrail) for Stuka to descend from (we used scaffold boards lashed between fixed lighting bars, accessed via the lighting gallery); that a responsible stage assistant is aloft throughout the operation to control the descent; that the abseil rope is securely anchored to a fixed point such as a roof beam; and that a safety harness is incorporated into Stuka's costume. (Lots of suitably Germanic straps and buckles shouldn't present a problem!)

If all else fails and you are unable to fly your Stuka in, then you may have to adopt a quite different approach. You could employ the sound effect of an aircraft rapidly descending, culminating in a crash landing — following which, Stuka could simply march on, dusting herself down. Alternatively, your Stuka could assume a 'Superman in flight' pose and be trundled majestically across stage mounted on a trolley pulled by wires! This may not have quite the same dramatic impact, but the comic possibilities are promising!

The Viking Longship

The original idea was to make a cartoon-like, two dimensional, cut-out ship, which would traverse the stage from one side to the other mounted on runners. Our technical supremo, however, got completely carried away with his cordless screwdriver, and actually ended up constructing the complete bow portion of a three-dimensional Viking longship! This consisted of a light timber framework rising to an eight foot high prow, surmounted by a fearsome stylized dragon head! The approximately boat-shaped frame was clad down to half an inch above stage floor level in strips of hardboard 'planking' which, once painted, appeared surprisingly realistic! The structure was mounted on several sets of concealed trolley wheels which allowed the ship to be slid forwards and backwards by its crew, standing two abreast inside. Round Viking shields were mounted along the gunwales, whilst the crew were equipped with ten foot long 'oars'. The shafts were rigid cardboard tubes from the centre of rolls of fabric, inset with long oar blades cut from hardboard.

After some practice, the crew became quite proficient at rowing their oars up and down in unison, whilst also slowly edging the longship forwards! Our ship thus advanced inexorably towards the audience from the stage (where it was preset behind the main tabs), and out on to a platform of stage blocks about twelve feet long by four feet wide — forming a sort of catwalk extending out into the auditorium. The improbable spectacle of this vessel emerging from a dense (smoke-machine generated) fog, oars dipping and rising in unison, accompanied by the ominous chanting of the half-seen, helmeted crew, and the suitably portentous swell of pseudo-Wagnerian music, triggered spontaneous applause from every audience that saw the show!

The ship was long enough to accomodate about a dozen crew. As there is no stern as such, you could also queue additional Vikings behind it. The audience really only perceive the foremost section of the ship — the remainder is purely illusory, especially if you are liberal with the smoke or dry ice!

One word of warning: the two actors taking the part of Big Rollo (one mounted on the other's shoulders) are in the longship when it first appears, and need to practise diligently to master the art of moving forward safely with the structure of the ship.

The Sleigh Crash

The final scene requires a sleighload of protagonists to smash through the wall of the villain's lair! Once again, this may sound a rather adventurous undertaking, but, in practice, it was surprisingly easy to achieve.

The wall, constructed from ubiquitous theatrical flats, was positioned to one side of the stage, leaving sufficient room behind to set the sleigh. The lower part of the wall was painted to resemble regular stonework, the upper part timber beams. It was decorated with hanging banners, swords, shields and so on. A four-foot square aperture was left at floor level in the centre of the wall, and this space was filled in with around forty cardboard boxes (approximately shoebox size), each artfully painted to resemble a stone block. Once stacked in place, this panel of cardboard 'stones' blended convincingly into the rest of the wall, and the audience only realized the deception when the sleigh smashed through the wall accompanied by a suitably cataclysmic sound effect!

The sleigh itself was built around a very low trolley, its wheels mounted on runners leading up to the aperture in the flats. This arrangement ensured that the vehicle was unable to deviate from a straight path to its destination! The trolley was propelled from a standing start to its terminal velocity of an impressive four miles per hour by the combined muscle power of the entire stage crew! Four miles per hour may not sound terribly fast, but it's sufficient to make the effect appear quite spectacular, as an apparently innocent area of stone wall suddenly dissolves into an explosion of rubble.

Although there are supposed to be ten people seated on the sleigh as it crashes through the wall, it is really only necessary for two or three to sit on board to convey the desired effect; the remainder can stagger in through the hole as the dust settles, having apparently tumbled off just before impact.

The prosaic reality is that with more than about three people on board, you will find the trolley almost impossible to move, much less propel at any speed, unless you are able to provide a long run-up, which, given the confines of most amateur stages, is highly unlikely!

The wall, complete with collapsible section, can either be preset before the performance or during the interval, and concealed behind legs.

Once again, do not feel obliged to adopt this method. You could use a painted panel of paper to smash through (which would have to be renewed after each performance) or you could even construct the entire wall of large polystyrene blocks, and bring the whole edifice down as the sleigh hits it!

Other Effects and Properties

More routinely, the action calls for the use of smoke or dry ice at certain points, several pyrotechnic flashes and bangs, one or two slightly unusual stage lighting effects, and a number of sound effects. Some of these elements could be omitted — although all contribute to the overall impact of the show.

You will also need to acquire or manufacture one or two unusual properties:

Hunting Horn. Unless you are able to lay your hands on a large 'Robin Hood'-style hunting horn, it is suggested that Svein's horn should be constructed from chicken wire covered in papier-mâché, painted black, then dry brushed with metallic paint to portray the appearance of beaten metal.

Trolley. Make sure that the trolley on which the trussed and helpless Radish is presented to Stoneheart has some form of brake — especially if your stage has a significant rake to it! And if you can't lay your hands on a tureen lid large enough to cover her, a crisp white tablecloth draped over will do just as well.

Skulls. Vikings supposedly quaffed mead from the trepanned skulls of their slain enemies. Human skulls are inexpensively available in 1:1 scale plastic kit form from most good model shops. The finished item is horribly realistic, and should represent a worthwhile addition to any amateur theatre group's properties store!

Music

There is provision in the script for about eight songs to be included, although the musical content can be varied according to taste, and the capabilities of the singers and musicians you have available. Feel free to incorporate additional songs — a crackpot duet for Smut and Helga in ACT II, SCENE 4 perhaps, or a comic song for Dame Dustpan with Tum, Dickon and Harald in ACT I, SCENE 3. In the original production we also had Smut and his Vikings lined up to perform a snarling but hilarious rendition of 'Do You

Smut's Saga

Want to Be in My Gang?' Mindful, however, of the impact lots of musical numbers can have on pace and the total running time of the show, we decided to spare our audiences this treat! Our production did feature comic pastiches of several chart toppers of the moment, as well as one or two Christmas pop classics! Although most lyrics were substituted for comic purposes, details are not given here for copyright reasons.

The inspired audience participation song 'Bash! Bash! Bash!' is entirely original however. So is the recommended 'Slushy Duet' (which Svein and Radish must deliver with absolutely straight faces!) The words and music are written by Mark Taylor, and reproduced in the present script by kind permission. The tunes are given on pp.74 and 76.

Richard Lloyd

Slushy duet

Music & Lyrics by Mark Taylor

Radish/Svein

1. We are two gol-den, rip-en-ing, sway-ing sheaves of sweet love. Wait-ing to be reaped by the scythe of to-geth-er-ness.
2. We are two ho-ney la-den bees just brim-ming with love. Mak-ing sweet hearts of gold in the air full of hap-pi-ness.

Cu-pid's oil-ing up his bow with gold-en trea-cle, sil-ver sy-rup and

joy. As the su-gar sweet - ly drips in-to our hearts, com -
15
bin - ing you and I.
Radish
The an - gel in the sky, with a
18
twin - kle in his eye,
Svein
He makes the
22
bright - est star shine out:
Radish/Svein
I love you.
26

Bash! Bash! Bash!

Music & Lyrics by Mark Taylor

I came a-cross a Vi-king who was bash-ing up my home, I took his club and bashed his arm and this is how it goes! Bash! Bash! Bash! Bash! Bash! Bash! Bash! Bash! Bash! Bash! Bash! Bash! Bash! Bash! Bash! Bash!

To repeat / **Last time**